How to Enhance Your Research

How to Enhance Your Research

100 Practical Tips for Academics

Don J. Webber

University of Sheffield, UK

Edward Elgar
PUBLISHING

Cheltenham, UK • Northampton, MA, USA

Published by
Edward Elgar Publishing Limited
The Lypiatts
15 Lansdown Road
Cheltenham
Glos GL50 2JA
UK

Edward Elgar Publishing, Inc.
William Pratt House
9 Dewey Court
Northampton
Massachusetts 01060
USA

Paperback edition 2022

A catalogue record for this book
is available from the British Library

Library of Congress Control Number: 2021946022

This book is available electronically in the **Elgar**online
Economics subject collection
http://dx.doi.org/10.4337/9781788978095

ISBN 978 1 78897 808 8 (cased)
ISBN 978 1 78897 809 5 (eBook)
ISBN 978 1 0353 0811 8 (paperback)

Printed and bound in Great Britain by TJ Books Limited, Padstow, Cornwall

Contents

Acknowledgements

FOR OUR ACADEMIC COMMUNITY

This project started as an opportunity to reflect on our collective ability to make the academic world a better place. Over the years, I have had informal discussions with friends, colleagues and acquaintances across different universities and it appears to me that some individuals perceive their institution to be demoralising and dispiriting while others see their institution as having a culture that is energising, supportive and enabling. The former group perceive their research activities as more of a chore while the latter group see their research as a source of happiness and something that they actively look forward to undertaking.

I wanted to understand what caused these differences in perceptions. Are they person-specific? Are perceptions common across individuals within an institution? For instance, an institution may be a place where academics bond by grumbling about things, and this grumbling feeds a scholastic atmosphere that enables research. When I talked through the positive and negative perceptions with respective individuals, I began to realise that they all wanted something multidimensional; they wanted:

- a persistent high valuation of research,
- to be recognised for researching something that had value to academia,
- to work in a research culture where they felt they could achieve their potential,
- to receive support from their research leaders, and
- the influence of negative colleagues to be suppressed.

Those friends, colleagues and acquaintances suggested many seemingly small initiatives that they saw could have huge beneficial effects on their own productivity, effectiveness and job satisfaction. This book is a collation of their uplifting ideas plus a sprinkling of my own. My hope is that this book moves forward the conversation about the academic research culture for the benefit of all.

My utmost thanks go to all of those friends, colleagues and acquaintances across a large number of institutions who provided me (directly, confidentially, candidly and/or overtly) with their insights, thoughts, guidance and advice, and opened up to share their innermost frustrations and feelings. I hope that it is understandable that I have avoided naming all of those wonderful individuals throughout this text. I appreciate fully their input into this project, without which it would not have come to fruition.

For added inspiration and/or comments on earlier drafts, I also thank Takara Christina, Sienna Mae, Naveena Prakasam, Annie Tubadji and Gail Webber. All errors are entirely my own.

Introduction: how can we enhance research?

Why are some academics more successful in their research activities than others? Are there activities that researchers can engage in that enhance the quality of their own and others' research? Can research leaders stimulate greater research output by their colleagues?

This book suggests good practice and makes recommendations that are designed to enhance your own and your colleagues' research potential and achievements. It is based on decades of experiences, observations, reflections, guidance, advice, and covert and overt practices and nudges that I experienced, observed, heard about or implemented. I have listened and learned from esteemed colleagues located at a variety of universities and research institutes, and I have tried to put many of these into practice as a professor, department research leader, head of department, interim head of department, researcher and as a colleague. This book summarises those tips, ideas and lessons with the hope of raising awareness that there are opportunities to purposefully and collectively increase the quality of our community's research output.

This book presents 100 tips and initiatives that can influence research behaviours and enhance academics' social norms. Some tips draw on conversations with researchers about their experiences, pleasures, frustrations, reflections and/or achievements at work. Some tips draw on conversations with researchers who recognise real and/or perceived barriers to and accelerators of their and others' research output. Some tips draw on my own experiences, while others are grounded on observations of departments that attempted, albeit based on goodwill, to impose structures designed to support research but which inadvertently hindered research.[1]

These practical tips and initiatives can be implemented by individual researchers and their research leaders. Many of these tips are simple and easy to put into practice, but they are frequently overlooked, trivialised, or not even recognised for their true benefits. When prioritised, they can culminate in enormous benefits for individual researchers and for the research culture within or across interconnected disciplines. Through this book, I hope to stimulate researchers and research leaders to discuss these initiatives with their colleagues in an attempt to enhance individual research activities and department research profiles and, most importantly, boost our speed and accuracy of understanding across the social sciences.

WHAT IS THE MAIN ARGUMENT OF THIS BOOK?

I will argue that we all need to frequently surround ourselves with people who challenge us in a supporting manner, make us hungry for knowledge, make us even more curious, provide the academic freedom to imagine the unimaginable, and positively motivate us. Research must be lived, and how you live it will influence the pace at which you improve; those who live their research the most will eventually become the senior and more recognisable leaders in their field. When researchers receive emotional and intellectual support, they feel more empowered, excited and energised to produce more and better-quality research. To progress you need both a network of support and the right personal attitude. Supportive, constructively critical working environments generate higher levels of employee well-being (Lopes, 2011)[2] and higher levels of well-being are experienced by individuals in organisations that facilitate autonomy and personal growth (Turban and Yan, 2016).[3]

Connected with this is the paradox of intention. Researchers who are happy and enjoy their research journey and possess intrinsically informed and achievable goals are likely to be the most productive. The important thing here is not that their happiness and motivation are linked to the achievement of those goals, but instead that their happiness and motivation are associated with *the journey* towards achieving those goals. For the journey to be enjoyable, the researcher needs to feel that the research has meaning, and for something to have meaning requires you to see its purpose. The purpose of your research lies integrally within you: you need to know what you are interested in most and what academic insights you wish to contribute in order to enjoy your journey. This is what keeps you going when you are knocked back by a desk rejection or an unfavourable referee report. Researchers should reflect on what gives them 'flow' in their journey – i.e. what gives them a mental state where they are fully engrossed in what they are doing with a feeling of energy, focus and undivided engagement – and they need to ensure that they know how to get that flow back when they lose it.

Once you have your flow, you will recognise that your job brings you the greatest amount of joy, and it will turn into a marvellous and engrossing hobby. You will enjoy progressing along the journey with others you have found along the way who are also fascinated by a topic. You could even synchronise your efforts, harmonise your activities and schedules, and socialise your research activities. Having colleagues who are progressing along a similar journey intensifies the feeling of purpose and personal flow. In *Thinking, Fast and*

Slow, Daniel Kahneman (2012)[4] banters that you can run 500 miles, but you can run 500 more miles if you are accompanied by your own 'Amos'.

Research leaders need to know how to help individuals remain in or return to their flow. Two of the most important things that I learnt about research are that (i) we have to enjoy the journey unreservedly in order to make an important contribution, and (ii) we should cultivate our research journey almost every day in order to ensure that we receive the creative and imaginative benefits of flow in our research lives. When you fully enjoy your research, and when you possess those intrinsic motivating forces, then you will be highly productive.[5] The more you enjoy something, the more you want to practise it; persistence reinforces practice; and the more you practise something, the better you get at it.[6]

We have all met academics who have been so demoralised and discouraged by poor management and administrative burdens[7] that they seem to accept that research is something that they will never have the capacity to undertake properly anymore; they seem to have given up and are resigned to a frustrating and unfulfilling academic career. Their flow has been disrupted so much that they do not believe they will ever experience it again. These colleagues need to surround themselves with uplifting and inspiring colleagues in order to give them hope that they will meet their aspirations.[8] Indeed, an insight of Maslow's (1943)[9] Hierarchy of Needs is that managers can shape the conditions that create a researcher's aspirations and drive to reach those aspirations. Throughout this book, I argue that it is not only a research leader's responsibility to create these conditions but also the responsibility of the researcher and the researcher's colleagues. This is the case not only for the achievement of the pinnacle of self-actualisation, but also for the general fulfilment and opportunities for personal and academic growth and development: research leaders are necessary for this effect but not sufficient because colleagues build on, refine and magnify the research leader's effect across the department.

If you are lucky enough to have the following research culture characteristics within your department, then you will know that you are able to feed off each other's enthusiasm and energy, iterate and nurture the research culture as a fuel for success, and create, maintain and enhance the department's research engine:

- ***intrinsically motivated*** academics who are dedicated to a cause,
- colleagues who have a group-centred (rather than individualistic) attitude and a strong sense of ***belonging*** to a part of their discipline,
- an attitude of ***support*** for research and for each other,
- an attitude of ***mutual respect*** for research and for each other, and
- an ***empowering*** attitude to undertake research with academic freedom.

This book suggests ways to install these research culture characteristics in your colleagues, conditional on them being open to receiving that guidance. It also suggests ways to enhance the belonging, intrinsic motivations, support, mutual respect and empowerment of academic researchers across a department.

Ask any successful researcher about how they achieved what they have done and they will typically answer in either or both of the following ways:

(i)   they have not yet achieved their potential because they are very inquisitive and there is so much more to learn and contribute to along their journey of discovery, and

(ii)   they have received vital feedback and guidance from peers, colleagues and a wider audience that has enabled them to identify their own oversights, and that social interaction and feedback has been of prime importance in enhancing their development.

Our greatest advisors who steer our research achievements, interests and abilities are our closest collaborators. They excel in giving supportive, critical, insightful and useful feedback. Yes, that feedback can be frustrating at times, perhaps excruciatingly so, but then sooner or later we realise that they make a well-meaning and insightful point, and that if we understand their feedback and respond to it appropriately then it will improve our work. What we achieve is in no small part because of the support we receive from our academic family.

> You cannot achieve efficiency or be fully effective by working on your own.

Recent investigations into why Sweden is a hotspot for innovation and technology, even though it has a population of only ten million citizens, reveal that this propensity may be related to the discouragement of extravagant displays of wealth, social opposition towards the revelation of success and the deconstruction of hierarchies. There appears to be greater needs-based collaboration and less competition in an environment where there are fewer competitive stress points,[10] when those stress points are performance enhancing[11] and when the feeling is that you are better off working at the same level as everyone else.[12] Similarly, a productive research group is one where there is togetherness in a clearly supportive team, with all researchers dedicated to reaching their goals, who use their academic freedom to pursue their research interests, who feel empowered to take the responsibility they need, and who encourage each other to do the same without any feelings of inferiority or concerns about their inability to compete. Active and prosperous researchers will value this collegiality (if they recognise it) and will not want to leave behind such a culture, as they would lose their identity and their source of happiness.[13]

WHOM IS THIS BOOK FOR?

This book has two main target audiences: first, I recommend this book to those who want to know how to improve the quality of their own research. This includes those new to social science research, those who have experienced a slowdown in their research output but want to reinvigorate it, and those who wish to publish in higher rank journals. Second, I strongly recommend this book to those with responsibility for enhancing the research output of their colleagues across the social sciences.

The greatest senior researchers that I have had the fortune to meet tend to be open, cooperative and approachable, and they informally undertake significant pastoral duties and covertly care for their colleagues. It is unfortunate, therefore, that many of these academics are too humble to take on formal head of department or research leader duties. These essential, primary researchers have expansive, informal networks and are the people researchers often go to for an informal chat, because that person is not judgemental of the person but is supportive, constructively critical and encouraging of research activities. It is my observation that excellent Heads of Department have exemplary and intricate prior knowledge of how to coordinate and enable their colleagues, and therefore recruitment of a Head of Department from outside the institution is inevitably going to be challenging for all.

This book is also for academics who want to know how to make other academics' work lives more enjoyable, and a significant part of this is the ability to allocate more quality time for lateral thinking. Lateral thinking requires frequent reflection and mental gymnastics about content and about the relevance of different perspectives; this requires a desire to immerse oneself into those perspectives and to assimilate the ideas.

Finally, this book is for those academics who enjoy their work and are already productive but wish to know how lucky they are and how to make it an equally enjoyable place to work for other up-and-coming and/or experienced researchers. When we achieve our 'flow',[14] research becomes a joyful journey. This flow galvanises us to push ourselves to our inventive extremes and to participate fully in research activities that can improve society.

WHY DO WE RESEARCH?

You do not undertake research activities simply for yourself; neither are you doing it simply for other researchers. You are undertaking research activities in order to help uncover and clarify knowledge. Once academics realise this, and it is resisted more in some disciplines than others, so the ceremonial component of knowledge creation is relegated and instead we stimulate and foster the instrumental part of research. Our modest contributions to the literature could enhance all of our understandings and make our knowledge and understanding of the world that tiny bit more comprehensive. Ever since Paine engaged with science and research and wrote his *Age of Reason*,[15] we have understood that this is the correct researcher mindset. We research and create scientific knowledge because we want to increase our collective understanding of the world; we do not conduct research simply to fulfil our personal curiosities.

In a supportive research culture, it is crucial to recognise that your colleagues are not your competitors! They are your co-workers and you all share a common goal, which is to uncover new knowledge. This book underscores the importance of building and maintaining a research culture and the importance of supportive, proactive and responsible behaviours by both individual researchers and research leaders in order to nurture and strengthen collegiate attitudes. Once you collectively create and maintain the appropriate set of research attitudes and behaviours, your department will obtain a research 'flow' – i.e. a particular collective state of mind[16] – where your research culture enables you to perform at your best and makes you a constructive element of the wider research community.

Finally, the book accentuates the vital role that a research leader performs in nurturing and improving their department, and it takes a personal touch (introverted[17] or otherwise) to create that productive research culture. Although the Internet and email have accelerated and improved our ability to connect with colleagues, it seems that these have driven an impersonal wedge between us, as we have reduced our prioritisation to connect meaningfully with each other with integrity and in a humanistic way.

NOURISHING MOTIVATIONS

The vast majority of academics did not enter the profession because they wanted to win a Nobel Prize or obtain some other type of critical acclaim. Most entered the profession because they realised that they were relatively good at something, that they were enormously interested in something and that they wanted to make a difference. This observation is nothing new: Dolan and Kudrna (2016)[18] emphasise that feelings of purpose and pleasure motivate our choices about what to do. Some motivations are intrinsic while others are extrinsic.

> The difference between a successful person and others is not a lack of strength, not a lack of knowledge, but rather a lack of will. (Vincent Lombardi)

In my experience, intrinsic motivations and genuine personal interest dominate and drive researchers' engagement in research activities, especially over the long run, albeit with a judicious sprinkling of external relevance. Unfortunately, the current trajectory of the academic system, especially within the UK but also across other predominantly English-speaking areas of the globe, seems to be towards escalating mechanisms that enhance extrinsic motivations, and this trajectory changes researchers' foci and reduces their natural and intrinsically driven engagement with and enthusiasm for their research.

Various studies reveal the behavioural effects of financial incentives[19] and highlight that any beneficial effect (when there is one) comes to an end in a short period of time. Frey (1993)[20] shows that extrinsic motivations crowd out the beneficial effects on productivity of high worker morale. Ariely et al. (2009)[21] emphasise that many understandings about incentives and policies are wrong, that the underlying assumptions regarding the mechanisms are seriously misguided, and that some extrinsic incentives actually have the reverse effect on productivity as they *reduce* effort. Ariely et al.'s results powerfully illustrate that financial (extrinsic) incentives *decrease* an individual's performance, and part of this is because it crowds out professional pride.

Most incentive structures also ignore and undermine the importance of morals. Creating personal financial reward systems or other structures designed to incentivise greater individual researcher productivity crowds out morals and intrinsic motivations for research, demoralises academics, splits departments into 'them and us', restricts academic progress, and constrains wider thought. This is consistent with the ideas of Samuel Bowles (2008),[22] who emphasises that incentives that appeal to self-interest fail when they undermine the moral values that lead people to act altruistically or in other public-spirited ways, which is a kind of negative synergy between economic incentives and moral behaviour. Specifically, Bowles (2008, p. 1605) argues that "economic incentives may diminish ethical or other reasons for complying with social norms and contributing to the common good" and that policies that appeal to economic self-interest affect the salience of ethical, altruistic and other social preferences.

Extrinsic incentives encourage researchers to work on tasks that are easy to monitor, such as recordings of publication output, rather than ones that are important for the substantive stock of knowledge, which are much harder to measure and often are not appreciated fully at the time of publication and therefore it is impossible to gauge their impact effectively at any point in time. For instance, the number of conference trips and associated costs can be easily measured by a research administrator, but the motivating effects of attending conferences and their spillover effects to a department's research culture cannot be measured with any accuracy and their impact fluctuates across departmental colleagues.

Some research seems to be produced simply to satisfy extrinsic motivations. Nosek et al. (2012)[23] and Smaldino and McElreath (2016)[24] argue that institutional incentive structures and the cultural transmissions of research practices lead to the production of research that has extremely negligible significance. Social forces encourage ceremonial conformity with a discipline's expectations of pedantic dexterity – such as the drive to visibly illustrate one's ability to present eloquent mathematical formulae – that do not necessarily assist in the advancement of real social science thought or practice, and can instead create a language that excludes others.

Ariely et al. (2011, p. 192)[25] argue that the presence of incentives illustrates that an institution does not trust the intrinsic motivations of its researchers to work effectively. Their research suggests that incentive mechanisms could even damage an organisation's performance because they may demoralise researchers who are seriously interested in improving our knowledge for society's benefit. Indeed, fuelling extrinsic motivations could damage research and innovation, especially if individual research activities driven by intrinsic motivations tend to help society. Famously, Titmuss (1970)[26] shows that paying people to donate blood broke established social norms about voluntary blood contributions and reduced the fraction of people wishing to donate blood. Similarly, breaking the link between researchers' intrinsic motivations and their social benevolence encourages researchers to be more selfish and myopic, and thereby reduces their prioritisation to produce research that benefits society.

Genuine intrinsically motivated interests fundamentally shape our levels of enjoyment of research activities and prevent us giving up on research ideas when they become too challenging. In contrast, extrinsic returns encourage us to make frequent, conspicuous and petite incremental achievements, in ever more complex ways, in order to gain recognition for numerous contributions. Extrinsic motivations do not encourage us to investigate something that is extremely meaningful and important to society, especially when the socially informed market for knowledge prioritises something else. Policies that create extrinsic rewards end up socialising the costs while privatising the benefits.

In my experience, most academic researchers are intrinsically motivated to contribute to society and to solve a socially beneficial problem, but trying to motivate them through extrinsic rewards can destroy this altruistic tendency and encourage them to produce output that contains conspicuous and ceremonial detail. It is my view that if we encourage behaviours that are consistent with carefully observed, socially benevolent and celebrated intrinsic motivations, then we can achieve greater good than if we use extrinsic motivations associated with metrics, ranks, monetary returns or other market-imposed structures.

MY SOAPBOX: SUPPORT AND ENCOURAGE

A university must have an institutional environment that values the cross-fertilisation of ideas and skills from experienced to less-experienced staff and back again. There are some institutions where the researcher is left to their own devices and is expected to produce research almost in isolation. In other institutions, the culture is so competitive that it frowns on collaborative and mutually supportive behaviour, often sourcing justification from research assessment exercise rules that state that a journal article can only be submitted under one resident researcher's name. These competitive cultures may be effective for some narcissistic researchers (and yes, such researchers definitely exist!), but knowledge production progresses much faster when people discuss their research openly, constructively and constructively critically, and when colleagues see mutual benefits from doing so. The act of providing constructively critical feedback to colleagues is grounded in the principal objective to improve the quality of the work. Furthermore, the best scholars actively learn from constructive criticism: they see the positives and appreciate the feedback.

The best research leaders, who combine generosity and compassion, already know that emotionally and intellectually supporting their colleagues takes a huge amount of time, energy, patience and perseverance; they also know that this effort pays off. Böckerman et al. (2020)[27] even find that there is a clear positive correlation between supervisory support and job control, with employee well-being negatively correlated with job-related stress. Research leaders (and heads of department) have a duty to understand what drives and enhances their colleagues' achievements and dedication, and the accumulation of this person-specific knowledge across a department requires a considerable amount of time. Research leaders must make time and must be given time to comprehend what their colleagues really need in order to excel, which sometimes is not what the junior researcher will necessarily demand. Bringing in a research leader or head of department from outside of a department or university should only be done if no other option is available and if a big structural change is required. Appointees from outside the department will require many months to be cognisant with the idiosyncratic intrinsic motivations of each and every colleague, and many of their efforts and achievements will inevitably be suboptimal.

We naturally adopt a research-leading, nurturing role when we mentor PhD students. Research leaders have the responsibility to nurture their colleagues, and this is why we are an academic family. Our best interests should be that all members of our family gain satisfaction from their efforts.[28] Moreover, as the best parents intuitively know, the support provided by research leaders to their colleagues must be selfless and reliable. A researcher should be given complete freedom to follow his or her own talent and intuition, and they should feel supported and not experience fear when they face a challenge or wish to proclaim an idea.

> Great minds discuss ideas. Average minds discuss events. (Anna Roosevelt)

Research leaders must be socially benevolent and want to get the best out of their colleagues. They should be actively interested in what their colleagues need, aware of what barriers (real or perceived) are in their colleagues' way and actively offer ideas to help. A research leader is there to guide their team forward while also leading by example. Proponents of self-determination theory, such as Deci and Ryan (2000),[29] argue that the conditions that incentivise intrinsic motivations are those that support autonomy, competence and relatedness. Nonetheless, actions that help one or a group of colleagues may be completely different to the actions that succeeded when a research leader was learning their trade. An effective and responsive research leader watches, listens, learns, understands, anticipates and reacts to the needs of their colleagues.[30] Much of what I advocate in this book is in line with the ideas of transformational leadership.[31] I advocate that research leaders need to:

- ensure that academic research (not externally funded research grants) is and remains the priority,
- raise awareness of the higher quality of academic work that can be achieved,
- encourage the mutually beneficial sharing of ideas,
- foster a culture of reciprocal support and respect, and
- coach using a supportive and encouraging language that is understood by everyone involved.

This means that the best research leaders:

- have a personal approach. They treat people as individuals and humans, not as machines or robots. Research leaders need to go above and beyond the norm to make sure people feel welcome, respected, and part of the team.
- recognise each colleague's potential and actual beneficial impact on the department. Academics are invariably people who want to make a beneficial difference and, if research leaders can explicitly recognise this in individuals, the colleague will feel valued and will contribute more to the team.[32] Some researchers will need this reassurance more than others, depending on their insecurity and self-esteem.
- talk to people verbally and face-to-face. Use Zoom or Skype if there is no alternative but be mindful that wholesome rapport is attained when you are in the same physical, relaxed and unconfrontational space. Personal

appreciation is communicated very poorly via email and can be embarrassing in meetings.

The best mentor and leader that I ever had was Professor Mike Campbell. Mike was an exemplar of a first-rate transformational leader who communicated very positive expectations to his colleagues and inspired, empowered and stimulated us all to exceed our levels of performance by nurturing our common interests, enthusiasm and motivations while challenging us to be innovative and creative. The humble and late Professor Mike Campbell was also an advocate in social justice and will forever be sadly missed.

The behaviours of those around you will shape your behaviours towards others. Of course, these lessons on how to interact with others commence and are learned in childhood, and then extend across our entire lives. Nevertheless, a researcher's early and updated experiences with their own research leaders will subsequently shape and revise their own interpersonal behaviours. A positive, nurturing and supportive experience with a research leader can fill you with joy and encourage you to help others, not for thanks or recognition but simply as a way of passing on the beneficial ambiances that have already been granted to you. This is how a healthy and constructively critical research culture reproduces itself in a sustainable, rewarding and expanding manner. Negative experiences with a research leader or senior member of staff (such as belittling, passive aggressiveness or gaslighting) will only encourage you to dismiss your colleagues' efforts, install in you an incorrect and shameworthy impression of superiority, and make you reticent to help others. Indeed, it appears that different disciplines have different cultures and therefore have different needs for this book.[33]

This book is unashamedly based on the belief that a department with a supportive and challenging (as opposed to undermining or gaslighting) leadership, which has a high degree of competence and values mutual respect, and where the environment is open, welcoming, non-hierarchical and constructively critical, is not only a convivial place to work but also one where research output thrives. This perspective is not new, as it has been forcefully promoted by Bland et al. (2005).[34] If you combine those work environment characteristics with unambiguous and clearly communicated goals, then research will flourish (Ryan and Hurley, 2007).[35] There are empirical findings which suggest that an environment with high workloads and a lack of institutional support for lateral thinking limits academic productivity,[36] while other findings emphasise that unfair leadership, role conflicts and inequality reduce research output.[37] Similarly, an institutional environment that promotes a climate of anti-intellectualism (Jacoby, 2009)[38] destroys lateral philosophical thought. Hence, academic policymakers interested in strengthening the production of research output should provide their researchers with a supportive and constructively critical workplace. A supportive culture was summarised by one of my former exemplary colleagues as

> the comfort of knowing you are well-considered, with full understanding of what you are, and with earnest care for your best. (Anon.)

Installing these values and norms in a department is difficult and changing a research culture for the better takes several years at a minimum and cannot be accomplished without the support and buy-in of senior colleagues. It cannot be achieved overnight as researchers' expectations and ways of working must evolve with the transition towards that supportive, open culture. When individuals in a department suffer from functional fixity and do not buy-in to a cultural transition, then transformational efforts will be ineffective.

> Intelligence is the ability to adapt to change. (Stephen Hawking)

Small changes can generate huge benefits (Thaller and Sunstein, 2008).[39] Senior and more experienced researchers must be willing and open to engage in the sharing of knowledge and the supporting of less experienced researchers. They must also be willing to use their experience to read and provide constructive and insightful feedback on their colleagues' manuscripts, and motivate and support colleagues by providing them with opportunities to discuss research in ways that constructively and usefully challenges their ideas in an utterly non-dismissive manner. Senior researchers need enough time and resources to be able to support their colleagues, as well as time to focus on writing their own research so that they can lead by example. Research leaders, therefore, need the utmost trust, respect and support of their own line managers too. Research leaders must be humble, approachable, resilient, persuasive, supportive and usefully critical towards their colleagues. Research leaders should use nuanced language intelligently when responding to the needs of individual colleagues, given those colleagues' personalities and temporal needs.

Experienced researchers need to collaborate with other experienced researchers too in order to keep their own research knowledge and tempo up to date. When experienced researchers collaborate visibly, their colleagues recognise that cooperation is a benevolent and mutually beneficial process. Learning to balance personal research and departmental leadership skills efficiently takes years of experience, but the promotion and appointment of someone as a research leader who does not have these skills only weakens the research culture. Benson et al. (2019)[40] emphasise that the best worker is not always the best candidate for a managerial position, and they question whether firms promote the best potential manager or the best worker in their current job. Research leaders must be experienced in academic research (some may say this is obvious, but I know it is not obvious to some). They also need to understand the trials and tribulations of academic research and be able to guide less experienced colleagues through these experiences, as without those experiences the research leader is unable to lead by example.

In some departments, research leaders feel threatened by their junior colleagues because they are worried that their junior colleagues will overtly challenge their superiority, and then they put those junior colleagues down rather than trying to inspire and encourage them. These people should not be promoted to leadership roles, as a true research leader should want their junior colleagues to surpass them (irrespective of that time delay), because the sign of a great research leader is when their less experienced colleagues progress quickly and rapidly improve the quality and impact of their research. Note that the important word is 'improve', which refers to a change rather than remaining at the same level irrespective of how high a level that is. Good research leaders create an inclusive culture that facilitates and enables their colleagues to improve at their optimal pace.

> I think that we can't go around measuring our goodness by what we don't do, by what we deny ourselves, what we resist, and who we exclude. I think we've got to measure goodness by what we embrace, what we create, and who we include. (Robert Nelson Jacobs)

Research leaders should want their colleagues to learn from their research leader's strengths and mistakes. Junior researchers, indeed all academic researchers, need someone to guide them and show them different ways of doing things. This guidance includes the provision of knowledge about what happens when mistakes are made, because it is only by making mistakes when pushing research boundaries forward that we eventually realise how to push boundaries in a more proficient manner. The avid and enthusiastic researcher who wants to improve their research should

- thoroughly embed themselves in the research culture,
- push their own boundaries and get things wrong no matter how uncomfortable those learning experiences can be,
- surround themselves with thinkers who are more imaginative than they are, and
- encourage colleagues to try to be better than they are, for it is only by surrounding yourself with more able colleagues that you are also able improve.

> If you are the smartest person in the room, then you are in the wrong room. (Michael Saul Dell)

At the individual level, it is not merely how good you are at research at a particular moment that is important, irrespective of the connotations of a research assessment exercise. Instead, we should actively consider how good you could become and what could be done to ensure that you achieve your potential. The most important role of a research leader is to ensure that all of their research colleagues are able to thrive.

It is similar at the department level: it is not how good at research you are collectively at a point in time that counts; it is about how good you all could become and what could be done to ensure that you all achieve your potential. The research atmosphere should be dynamic and forward thinking, with a clear purpose and implementation strategy that enhances quality and the sustainable growth of policy-relevant research. We have a responsibility as academic scholars to commit to do our individual and collective best and to repay society's support and investment in our education and training through the advancement of knowledge and understanding.

TREAD WITH CARE

Senior research staff (research leaders and all fellow professors) shape the research atmosphere within a department. Their role is to lead by example, be open to collaboration, provide constructive feedback and offer support to all of their colleagues (irrespective of differences in ontological or epistemological approach), and, very importantly, have their doors open to welcome all colleagues should they require help or advice. The actions of senior research staff can either enable their colleagues to excel and succeed, or unwittingly discourage and demoralise them so they underperform.

Senior research staff should take credit and immense pride when a department improves under their collective leadership. Senior research staff should also take the collective blame when their department is not performing, when either the policies or actions need to change, or the research leaders need to change.

Some researchers need their colleagues to open doors for them, while other researchers barge through the doors themselves. Given the appointment of senior staff with different research backgrounds,[41] interests and networks, it is impossible for the mix of senior staff members to be able to open an informed range of doors for all of their colleagues. When a colleague perceives others receive more help than they do, a sense of disadvantage and unfairness can permeate through a department. Control of that damaging narrative is imperative and requires cooperation[42] across all of the senior staff who should distinguish those divisive (conscious or otherwise) behaviours and reunite their department so that they work together in a supportive manner once again.

Research leaders and other senior researchers could stop opening doors for their colleagues just in case some feel relatively disadvantaged or discouraged by a perception that they are receiving less support. However, this would be totally the wrong thing to do. Research leaders should be visibly opening doors for as many of their colleagues as possible, but they should be clear that they have tried when some doors remain shut or when they did not see an opportunity. All colleagues need to know that doors open episodically, and it can be a period of time until the right doors open. Patience is a virtue, but also required is the belief and acceptance that senior colleagues are proactively supporting all colleagues, without exception. Unfortunately, some colleagues will not believe and accept this, rightly or wrongly, and become combative to stake a claim.

Of course, people's insecurities and neediness do vary over time and this can be unpredictable and even unobservable if the research leadership staff do not know their colleagues well enough; even if they do notice a change in behaviour then they may misinterpret that change. These leaders need to have the capacity and the personality to listen properly to their colleagues and then be responsive to their needs either by focusing on opening more doors for them or by correcting misconceptions.

Opening different doors brings different benefits to different colleagues but often in unforeseeable ways. It is important that people are aware that support is available and provided, and that senior staff are working to help them realise their potential. When people do not feel supported, which can be different to the support that they really receive, then that is when they often decide to leave and join a competitor research institution.

MAKING EVERYONE SUCCESSFUL

There are four levels of interwoven responsibilities that collectively generate an excelling research culture. First, it is the responsibility of senior researchers to create a supportive research culture. Second, the primary responsibility for all researchers is to create high-quality substantive research outputs. There are many ways to achieve a successful research career, and these seem to vary within and across disciplines, the position within a career and the levels of enthusiasm for the topic by the researcher and by others. Third, once you feel that you are making progress in your research, the next step is for you to enable your peers to develop their own research by helping to remove any barriers that inhibit their progress. Fourth, and the pinnacle of any highly active research department, is to ensure that everyone supports and helps each other by, for example, taking the time to read and provide feedback on each other's research. These stages are hierarchical and sequential, as shown in the

Research Pyramid illustration (Figure 0.1), with the pinnacle being that all colleagues actively support each other's research activities.

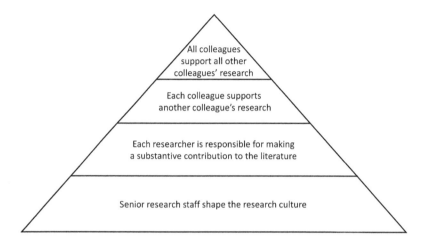

Figure 0.1   The Research Pyramid

It is possible that the bottom two layers of the Pyramid are interchangeable, where researchers take responsibility for their own research and then collectively shape the research culture; this can work when the research leader and senior staff members do a poor job in creating a beneficial research atmosphere. It is also possible that the top two levels change order, and this is where everyone helps their colleagues, and this can change the behaviour of a colleague who is naturally selfish and self-absorbed so that they wake up and support their colleagues by following their example. The latter can also occur when a new member of staff joins a department. Part of this ordering is driven by the strength of social norms within the department.

A researcher should be promoted to a leadership role only if they have the skills and ability to construct an effective and supportive research culture. However, this key research leadership skill seldom seems to be the principal concern of those who decide who should lead a group of researchers. Instead, it is often the case that someone is promoted as a reward for their own research achievements rather than their ability to enable others to develop.[43]

It is possible that the achievements of the research leader are not of the type that others in the department value or respect (such as a trade-off between income generation and quality academic publications). A mismatch between types of achievement and research values will affect perceptions of the importance of particular types of research and can lead colleagues to perceive that their own research is no longer valued. Satisfaction levels of a leading researcher is important for the external recognition of the department, especially when they are attempting to recruit new high-flying staff, but the development and future achievements of a research group are ultimately influenced by the morale and job satisfaction of other researchers within the group.[44]

David Spencer's (2015)[45] insightful investigations into the satisfaction of work emphasises that it is not just the work that is important for the individual but also the context and organisation of the work that makes it meaningful. Vice Chancellors, Faculty Deans and Associate Deans need to decide on and shape the type of research culture that they want within their faculties and departments, and then recruit appropriate research leaders to implement that culture, perhaps driven by their desire to make a change.[46] For instance, do these senior persons want to create a community of practice[47] or a set of competing individuals? A successful research-focused team needs to work together effectively with a united front for the greater good.

NEWTONIAN VERSUS DARWINIAN DEVELOPMENT

So how do researchers get better at what they do? How do they become great at research? There are two contrasting yet dominant perspectives in this literature. The pedagogical perspective states that someone purposefully learns something, applies those ideas, reapplies those ideas and becomes more efficient and more effective at doing so. Some lawyers, contract researchers, scientists, etc. do it this way: they learn the path and then apply those ideas. This Newtonian stance works for some, but it is not the guidance that I would give to post-doctoral social scientists who aspire to make a tangible contribution to society.

The alternative dominant perspective is that you do not simply learn and relearn something; instead, you need to draw on self-reflection in order to extricate yourself from your normal stance and disentangle yourself from your own biased assumptions. You need your colleagues to point out those gaps that you were not aware existed. You learn from others who think differently from yourself. You need to merge new information with what you already know, and then use this new knowledge to push forward your own social scientific investigations. In other words, researchers should remain free, responsible and self-critical in order to conceive and develop their own ideas. Similarly, they need to aid and supportively stimulate the rumination of their colleagues' ideas.

The former perspective pushes the research path forward, but not necessarily in the direction of interest to the researcher; it is useful for contract research, is functional and can be instrumental, but it does not necessarily make a substantive contribution to the development of knowledge. Instead, try to ensure that you make substantive contributions to the literature. Researchers need time for reflection as well as the presence of supportive and constructively critical feedback that pushes us in the direction that we are intrinsically motivated to investigate. We need to be reminded what is worth doing, what is important, what is interesting, what is useful for society and what is pedantic. There is a place in academia for purely academic research in the same way that there is space for purely practice-oriented research. We need people to observe our research, and to provide us with constructively critical feedback, to nudge us in the right direction even when that nudge can feel uncomfortable.

> Start with what is right rather than what is acceptable. (Franz Kafka)

Seemingly randomly occurring nudges can be very uncomfortable experiences, sometimes embarrassingly so, and can make us not want to do something again. Subsequent reconsideration of those nudges with a reflective mind can help us move in the right direction and will make us stronger ... eventually. Some colleagues, even if they have their heart in the right place, will appear to be trying to gain brownie points by belittling us when we present an open talk, such as in a staff seminar or during a conference speech. Those belittling colleagues do this because they need to feel superior to you, and that is because they lack self-worth. Some academic conference circuits even have this type of behaviour engrained in their culture.[48] People in the audience will know that an arrogant delegate in the audience is being a jerk when they ask and phrase a particular question in a derogatory way; those audience members will reticently take pity on the presenter but may not admit to it due to social pressures to conform to an academic culture. Nevertheless, the vast majority of people in the audience will be on your side and will want you to learn from the mistakes that we all make from time to time, because they have been in your position too, and because they will have learned from the experience irrespective of how small the experience made them feel.

> What doesn't kill you makes you stronger. (Genghis Kahn)[49]

Irrespective of how good or bad the people are around you, try to find the power within yourself to recognise and embrace healthy criticism whenever it comes your way. When you have the trust of your research mentor who believes unreservedly in your capability and what you will achieve eventually, then you should have the belief that you can develop and progress.[50] After all, some of the most powerful lessons to learn in life are only presented in the form of setbacks.

The greatest glory in living lies not in never falling, but in rising every time we fall. (Nelson Mandela)

STRUCTURE OF THIS BOOK

This book has ten sections with each section containing ten tips. The first section highlights indispensable points that are vital for a strong research career and for an active, supportive and constructively critical research culture. These ten tips may appear trivial and second nature to established researchers who are based in departments that already have these characteristics, but they are all too easy to lose sight of, trivialise, ignore and not value. These are things that the department should support, get right as a priority and install as habits in all of their colleagues.

The next three sections highlight practices that individual researchers should engage in, and which research leaders should encourage. It is paramount that the research leader consistently reflects on whether their colleagues are practising these good behaviours and appraise whether there is anything they can do to strengthen these activities.

The following three sections focus on the benefits of collaboration and the wide range of collaborative covert and overt behaviours that exist when giving and receiving support and advice. The last three sections focus on the leveraging of benefits for research from teaching, external grant capture and knowledge exchange. If these activities are carried out efficiently and effectively, there are enormous benefits for the researcher, for their research trajectory and for the benefit of society. However, if these interconnections are misunderstood, if external funders exploit their incentivising position or if the researcher gets distracted by other newly found initiatives, external grants and knowledge exchange activities can be at a cost to their own and their department's research trajectory. The lessons provided within those three sections could help drive forward even the best research-active departments.[51] Each tip is discussed first by stating the idea and what is good practice. Each tip then proceeds by stating why this is good practice and when this practice should be implemented. Emphasis is placed on how a research leader can enable and encourage these practices within the department. Note that each of these three segments varies in importance depending on the topic, and this is reflected in the text.

A research leader can stimulate and motivate research-active colleagues, and they can construct soft supportive structures that integrate staff into a collaborative culture. However, they can also destroy soft, motivating and supportive structures, which can then extinguish a research culture and reduce researchers' confidence, and thereby depress research output and researcher flow. A positive research culture takes years to build and a short time to wipe out.

Real positive step change in research and in a research culture occurs when people interact and help each other. We need productive disagreement, as real progress and creativity depend on it. But disagreement does not mean that we should tolerate incivility; quite the opposite, as we are more likely to listen, acknowledge, recognise unintended consequences and even comprehend an awareness of contending perspectives when we are civil.

I hope you find this book useful, but if you do not find it useful, and that may be because you already run or work in a successful research-focused department or because you disagree with the importance of these tips, then please pass this book on to someone who could benefit from it. If you and/or your department are not achieving what you had hoped for, then perhaps the good practices that you thought were installed in the behaviour of yourself and of your colleagues are not being adopted effectively, or followed closely enough, or maybe that structure is the wrong one for your colleagues. Perhaps your department is too competitive and not collaborative enough.

Finally, to develop as a researcher and as a research-focused department you need to have the right balance between individual and collective attitudes. A first-class and high-achieving department will have a research culture based on a collection of attitudes that nurtures and reproduces a genuine drive for knowledge for the common good. That is why we should help each other to perform at and achieve our best, to rediscover our best when we lose it, and to reinforce each other's enjoyment and interests in a topic and in our journey together.

Good luck !!

Figure 0.2   The Research Wordcloud

NOTES

1. This book does not present the results of a research project that sought to identify the dynamic implications of particular policies to enhance research; given the enormity of such a project, it would inevitably have been case- or time-specific.
2. Lopes, H. (2011), 'Why do people work? Individual wants versus common goods', *Journal of Economic Issues*, 45(1), pp. 57–73.
3. Turban, D. B. and Yan, W. (2016), 'Relationship of eudaimonia and hedonia with work outcomes', *Journal of Managerial Psychology*, 31(6), pp. 1006–20.
4. Kahneman, D. (2012), *Thinking, Fast and Slow*, Penguin Books.
5. If you do not enjoy your research, then you will never reap the rewards of flow in your research. Flow will not come to you when you are discontented or demoralised; you will not achieve your research potential; you will not achieve that four-star publication that you yearn for; you may even stop yearning for improvement because you begin to believe that you will never achieve it. If your happiness is not present, then your flow will be lost. Do not be trapped in a job that you absolutely hate – it will drain you of all energy, enjoyment and fulfilment, and you will be letting yourself down, your favoured research career down, your department down, your discipline down, and society will not be able to benefit from your research. Know when it is time for a change. The difficulty, of course, is finding a better and convenient alternative. Ultimately, you only excel at what you enjoy.
6. Notice that when our motivation wanes, and motivation comes and goes, we end up only doing the easiest things that require the least amount of effort. See Carter, C. (2021), 'The 1-minute secret to forming a new habit', TED Talk, https://www.ted.com/talks/christine_carter_the_1_minute_secret_to_forming_a_new_habit#t-379977.
7. If line managers increase workloads or impose new things to do that are not consistent with a researcher's main interests or skill set, then the repercussion will be a lower quality or lower quantity of research. Differences in workloads may be an important reason for the gap in research quality and research output between research-intensive and teaching-intensive universities. After all, it is not where you trained for your doctorate that matters for your research output, but where you work. See Way, S. F., Morgan., A. C., Larremore, D. B. and Clauset, A. (2019), 'Productivity, prominence, and the effects of academic environment', *Proceedings of the National Academy of Sciences of the United States of America*, 116(22), pp. 10729–33. If teaching-intensive universities want to increase their research output, they must stop giving those researchers new or more duties.
8. Poggi (2010) argues that the personal gap between how we feel we are doing and what we aspire to do is what drives job satisfaction. See Poggi, A. (2010), 'Job satisfaction, working conditions, and aspirations', *Journal of Economic Psychology*, 31(6), pp. 936–49.
9. Maslow, A. H. (1943), 'A theory of human motivation', *Psychological Review*, 50(4), pp. 370–96.
10. Amy Milton is a behavioural neuroscientist and argues in her TED Talk that high levels of stress stop us storing details of events. See https://www.ted.com/talks/amy_milton_can_we_edit_memories?language=en. It is possible that researchers under high levels of stress may not focus on the what,

where and when effectively enough. Ensuring that a researcher is under a low level of stress may enable them to achieve their potential faster.

11. Akinola, M. and Wilson, R. (2020), 'Train yourself to shine under stress', TED Talk, https://podcasts.apple.com/us/podcast/train-yourself-to-shine-under-stress -russell-wilson/id470622782?i=1000502290737.
12. See BBC (2018), 'Is boasting good or bad for business?' www.bbc.co.uk.news/ business-43060675.
13. Of course, this is consistent with Maslow's (1943) idea that the social value of cooperation itself can fulfil human needs. See Maslow, A. H. (1943), 'A theory of human motivation', *Psychological Review*, 50, pp. 370–96.
14. For an excellent book on the connections between flow and happiness, see Csikszentmilalyi, M. (2002), *Flow: The Psychology of Happiness*, Rider Publishers.
15. Paine, T. (2009 [1794]), *The Age of Reason: The Complete Edition*, World Union of Deists.
16. See Freud, S. (2012 [1921]), *Group Psychology and the Analysis of the Ego*, Empire Books.
17. See Kahnweiler, J. (2018), *Introverted Leader: Building on Your Quiet Strength*, Berrett-Koehler Publishers.
18. Dolan, P. and Kudrna, L. (2016), 'Sentimental hedonism: pleasure, purpose and public policy', in Vittersø, J., *Handbook of Eudaimonic Well-Being*, Springer.
19. See, for instance, Kane, R. L., Johnson, P. E., Town, R. J. and Butler, M. (2004), 'A structured review of the effect of economic incentives on consumers' preventive behaviour', *American Journal of Preventative Medicine*, 24, pp. 327–52.
20. Frey, B. S. (1993), 'Shirking or work morale? The impact of regulating', *European Economic Review*, 37(8), pp. 1523–32.
21. Ariely, D., Gneezy, I., Loewenstein, G. and Mazar, N. (2009), 'Large stakes and big mistakes', *Review of Economic Studies*, 76, pp. 451–69. Ariely is an example of a person deeply intrinsically engaged with his topic for personal reasons and at the highest professional standard. This is the best mix of engagement where heart and mind are together.
22. Bowles, S. (2008), 'Policies designed for self-interested citizens may undermine "The Moral Sentiments": evidence from economic experiments', *Science*, 320(5883), pp. 1605–9.
23. Nosek, B. A., Spies, J. R. and Motyl, M. (2012), 'Scientific utopia', *Perspectives on Psychological Science*, 7(6), pp. 615–31.
24. Smaldino, P. E. and McElreath, R. (2012), 'The natural selection of bad science', *Royal Society Open Science*, 3, 160384. This can be accessed at https://ro yalsocietypublishing.org/doi/pdf/10.1098/rsos.160384
25. Ariely, D., Meier, S. and Rey-Biel, P. (2011), 'When and why incentives (don't) work to modify behavior', *Journal of Economic Perspectives*, 25(4), pp. 191–210.
26. Titmuss, R. M. (1970), *The Gift Relationship*, Allen and Unwin.
27. Böckerman, P., Bryson, A., Kauhanen, A. and Kangasniemi, M. (2020), 'Does job design make workers happy?' *Scottish Journal of Political Economy*, 67(1), pp. 31–52.
28. There is no point in being a rotten kid; see Becker, G. S. (1981), *A Treatise of the Family*, Harvard University Press.
29. Deci, E. L. and Ryan, R. M. (2000), 'The "what" and "why" of goal pursuits: human needs and the self-determination of behaviour', *Psychological Inquiry*, 11(4), pp. 227–68.

30. These issues are in addition to the Peter and Paula Principles. See Schuller, T. (2017), *The Paula Principle: How and Why Women Work Below Their Level of Competence*, Scribe; Peter, L. J. and Hull, R. (1969), *The Peter Principle: Why Things Always Go Wrong*, William Morrow and Co.

31. See Burns, J. M. (2004), *Transformational Leadership: A New Pursuit of Happiness*, Grove Press.

32. See Robert Reffkin's TED video for an upbeat and short summary. This can be accessed at https://www.ted.com/talks/robert_reffkin_5_ways_to_create_stronger _connections#t-157396.

33. For instance, on 9 February 2020, the American Economic Association sent an email to its members to state that it had "taken several important steps to improve the professional climate in economics. As part of this continuing effort, today I am pleased to report on establishing a set of guidelines for investigating complaints that officers and/or members of the Association have violated the Association's Code of Conduct and Policy on Harassment and Discrimination. The AEA Code of Professional Conduct, adopted by the Executive Committee in April 2018 after consultation with the membership, was supplemented by a more detailed Policy on Harassment and Discrimination, also ratified by the Executive Committee. Acknowledgment and acceptance of both the Code and the harassment and discrimination policy is now required for participation in any AEA-sponsored activity or committee. During 2019, AEA members voted to amend the AEA bylaws to add a provision so that a member and/or officer who violates the Code or the Policy may be sanctioned or membership may be terminated as voted by a two-thirds majority vote of the Board of Trustees. The amended bylaws can be read in their entirety at https://www.aeaweb.org/resources/member -docs/certificate-of-incorporation-bylaws. The new guidelines for investigating complaints, and, if necessary, imposing sanctions, have been approved by the Executive Committee and are effective immediately. They are posted on the AEA website at https://www.aeaweb.org/go/policy-hd/procedures. Instructions for filing formal complaints with the Association's Ethics Committee, and for consulting with the AEA Ombudsperson about potential complaints, are also available at https://www.aeaweb.org/go/policy-hd/formal-complaint and https://www.aeaweb .org/about-aea/aea-ombudsperson/faq. The Association remains committed to improving the professional climate in economics and considers the adoption of these guidelines another important step in helping make my field accessible and welcoming to anyone with the interest and ability to make a career in it. I ask for the support of all members in these efforts."

34. Bland, C. J., Center, B. A., Finstad, D. and Staples, J. G. (2005), 'A theoretical, practical, predictive model of faculty and department research productivity', *Academic Medicine*, 80(3), pp. 225–37.

35. Ryan, J. and Hurley, J. (2007), 'An empirical examination of the relationship between scientists' work environment and research performance', *R&D Management*, 37(4), pp. 345–54.

36. Clarke, M., Kenny, A. and Loxley, A. (2015), 'Creating a supportive working environment for academics in higher education', *Country Report Ireland*, The Teachers' Union of Ireland and Irish Federation of University Teachers, Dublin.

37. Lohela-Karlsson, M., Hagberg, J. and Bergström, G. (2014), 'Production loss among employees perceiving work environment problems', *International Archives of Occupational and Environmental Health*, 88(6), pp. 769–77.

38. Jacoby, S. (2009), *The Age of American Unreason*, Vintage Books.

39. Thaler, R. and Sunstein, C. (2008), *Nudge*, Penguin Books.
40. Benson, A., Li, D. and Shue, K. (2019), 'Promotions and the Peter principle', *Quarterly Journal of Economics*, 134(4), pp. 2085–134.
41. A very interesting result is reported by Way et al. (2019) who show that the scientific productivity of academics depends not on where they trained for their doctorate but instead on where they work; it is therefore the workplace that shapes and nurtures talent and enables colleagues to achieve, and not where they studied their degrees. See Way, S. F., Morgan, A. C., Larremore, D. B. and Clauset, A. (2019), 'Productivity, prominence, and the effects of academic environment', *Proceedings of the National Academy of Sciences of the United States of America*, 116(22), pp. 10729–33.
42. The moral valence of cooperative behaviour is uniformly positive; see Curry, O. S., Mullins, D. A. and Whitehouse, H. (2019), 'Is it good to cooperate? Testing the theory of morality-as-cooperation in 60 societies', *Current Anthropology*, 60(1), pp. 47–69.
43. These issues are in addition to the Peter and Paula Principles. See Schuller (2017), *The Paula Principle*; Peter and Hull (1969), *The Peter Principle*.
44. The BBC writes (https://www.bbc.co.uk/sport/football/51962924) that the reason Wolverhampton Wanderers Football Club are competing to be sixth in the English Premier League is because its manager, Nuno Espírito Santo, has a focus on team morale and team bonding. Since the start of his coaching career, the Portuguese manager has placed great emphasis on tight-knit squads. There has been an emphasis on creating a small, unified group of players to make up the first team and his awareness of the importance of keeping everyone involved is likely to be a consequence of his own playing experience. Keeping all of the squad onside is an important part of Nuno's philosophy and his office is always open to those seeking advice or to discuss any part of football or life. (22 March 2020).
45. Spencer, D. A. (2015), 'Developing an understanding of meaningful work in economics: the case for a heterodox economics of work', *Cambridge Journal of Economics*, 39, pp. 675–88.
46. Teaching-focused institutions will prioritise enhancing their teaching provision using structures designed to ensure high-quality teaching. Research-focused institutions will prioritise academic research and compete for prestigious research funds to compete in the international rankings of research-intensive universities. Other institutions will prioritise income generation, especially when they do not have a particular strength in either teaching or academic research. Increasingly, academic institutions are trying to compete in two or all three of these areas, thereby putting additional pressure on staff.
47. See https://www.advance-he.ac.uk/knowledge-hub/communities-practice. See also Lave, J. and Wenger, E. (1991), *Situated Learning: Legitimate Peripheral Participation*, Cambridge University Press; Kimble, C., Hildreth, P. and Bourdon, I. (2008), *Communities of Practice: Creating Learning Environments for Educators*, Information Age Publishing.
48. For one potential example of many, see note 33.
49. Alternatively, Friedrich Nietzsche famously said, "That which does not kill you, makes you stronger."
50. When Adrián San Miguel del Castillo (known as Adrián) moved to Liverpool Football Club on a free transfer on 5 August 2019, it was a surprise to many that he made his debut after being at the club for only four days when he replaced Allison (the club's first-choice goalkeeper) after 39 minutes due to an injury to

Allison. Writing on the BBC website and responding to the interviewer's question of "did Klopp have anything else to add [when he was about to make his debut]?", Adrián states that "He hugged me. He showed me I had his trust ... the way the fans embraced me in such a critical moment ... They gave me total confidence." Commenting further about Jürgen Klopp, Adrián continues by saying, "It is so easy working with him. So easy. He's always smiling, cheerful, optimistic. ... He's there to guide us. He visualises football very well from the sidelines and transmits this knowledge to the players in a masterful way." Clearly this approach can work in a variety of settings. This is consistent with empirical findings that optimism fuels social cooperation (Oyediran et al., 2018) and that cooperation can enhance productivity. See Oyediran, O. A., Rivas, M. F., Coulson, M. and Kernohan, D. (2018), 'Cooperation and optimism in social dilemma', *Bulletin of Economic Research*, 70(4), 335–40.

51. This is the case in the UK where we will soon have a Knowledge Exchange Framework (KEF) in addition to the Teaching Excellence and Student Outcomes Framework (TEF) and the Research Excellence Framework (REF).

PART I

The essentials

We can easily lose sight of the essentials discussed in this section. We sometimes assume that because we adopted a best practice research approach in the past, then we can easily return to that practice when we need to, such as during non-teaching weeks. However, research is an ongoing iterative process, and the longer the time gaps between quality research engagements then the poorer will be our ability to re-engage effectively and productively in our research activities. Quality research is not achieved in 20-minute intervals every now and again and according to a timetable; it is cumulative and episodic and requires frequent immersion. There is no effective structure to successful academic research other than ensuring that it is an activity that we experience frequently.

Best practices can easily go by the wayside when we allow other responsibilities to take priority. Often, we do not fully appreciate the impacts that these other responsibilities, such as teaching or administrative duties, can have on our research activities. If we allow other responsibilities to impinge on our research time too much, it can lead to a slippery slope with an ever-decreasing quantity of research time.

One simple way to identify how much quality research time you have undertaken is to make a record of time spent on research activities. This can provide you with a reality check and an indication about why your research progress is slower than you want it to be. It can encourage you to reflect on your priorities and provide you with an evidence base on which you can decide whether you need to change something. If you realise that time is not the issue, the reasons for a poor research record may lie elsewhere. Of course, we all wish to have more time for our research, but there are things that we can do collectively that help each other along our research journeys and can improve our research achievements without requiring a substantial increase in research time.

1.   Read a lot!

Many academics do not prioritise reading journal articles and keeping up to date with the literature. We all have competing demands on our time; if it is not teaching then it is teaching preparation, designing an appropriate research method, writing up results, redrafting papers, discussing ideas with co-authors, preparing to present research, etc.

Reading stimulates you mentally and gives you knowledge. It encourages you to make links between areas of knowledge that you might not have done before. The longer the period of time that you do not read, the further you will fall behind the literature. Reading also updates contrasting arguments and can strengthen your analytical skills. Reading also improves your understanding of how to write an argument, and it will help you hone your writing skills. Do not only read papers in your particular research area, as reading around your subject area will enable you to re/discover what people are doing in other connected research areas, and those ideas may spill over into your own research area. Be cognisant of new methodological advancements and new ways of thinking. Read journals in connected disciplines (e.g. economists should read sociology and anthropology) to stimulate your mind to juggle contrasting thoughts. Read newspapers to discover examples. Read some old literature that may have been undervalued through the ages – you might imagine a contemporary understanding of a not hitherto appreciated idea.

Read one paper every working day. If you enjoy it, then reading can help you relax. Sometimes the best time of the day to read is before you embark on your other duties. Some like to read immediately after lunch while others find it difficult to read after eating when they may feel drowsy and inattentive. Do not read so much that it stops you from writing or discussing content with others; after all, reading should complement your own writing, not replace it. Try to fit some reading into every working day and be flexible on the choice of paper depending on the amount of time that you have available; some papers are short and will only take 30 minutes to read while others will require much more time for cogitation. Do not try to shoehorn a complex paper into an hour's slot if this time constraint limits your ability to read and understand it fully.

Research leaders could organise reading groups to encourage colleagues to draw out lessons from important papers. A good place to start is Ziliak and McCloskey's (2008)[1] view on the *Cult of Statistical Significance*. Challenging texts stimulate lively, focused debate and greater knowledge sharing and engagement between colleagues. Research leaders should encourage colleagues to suggest texts that they think are important or contentious. They can also suggest texts that they wish to know others' perspectives on. Not everyone within a department will be interested in the same literature, so membership of reading groups should be fluid and inclusive, and address broad topics. If there are papers that a research leader thinks could be useful for specific colleagues, they should highlight those papers to their colleagues. The next step is for the research leader to emphasise to their colleagues that they would be interested in their perspective on a paper, and this would make the colleagues feel stimulated and respected.

NOTE

1.   Ziliak, S. T. and McCloskey, D. N. (2008), *The Cult of Statistical Significance*, University of Michigan Press.

2.   Write something every day

Try to write something on your research topic every working day. There will be days when you literally can't write anything because of other demands on your time, but even if you write for only 30 minutes per day, those 30 minutes will slowly accumulate into something substantial and ensure that your research idea does not weaken in your mind. Writing something almost every working day will mean that the topic remains fresher in your mind and you will be able to return to the crux of your research question much quicker the next time you have a serious amount of quality time to devote to your research.

Writing leads to more writing and writing with more freedom and imagination. The avoidance of writing snares you and restricts your ability to strengthen a contribution and form a cohesive argument. Frequent writing and redrafting improve your ability to construct arguments with clarity.

New academics tend not to fully appreciate the importance of the clarity of the argument, and your ability to write will steadily improve over time if you put in the time to practise. Your ability to construct the argument will improve the more you return and redraft the text and build in lessons learned from your reading.

Do you ever read papers in the highest quality journal outlets and realise that the argument is so simple that you could have written it? Yes, what a shame that you didn't! It can be the extreme clarity of an argument that convinces the editor and referees that an idea is strongly conceptualised, developed and expressed in a way that any reader will be able to understand. What is often not fully appreciated, however, is that the extreme clarity of argument in papers in top journals is a reflection of years or decades of practise, synthesis, reflection and redrafting. Well-presented research makes the research look easy to do and easy to understand, but this takes huge amounts of practise, drafting and redrafting.

Unfortunately, if you don't practise writing regularly, your ability to write clearly and concisely will suffer, and people who do not write regularly will find it very difficult to restart the writing process after a period of time away from it. Rewriting your scripts will improve the clarity of your arguments to you and most probably to your readers too, and it is the latter that is vitally important.

Rewriting text can stimulate new ideas and help you think laterally and creatively. Sometimes new ideas percolate naturally in your mind when you rephrase, reconstruct and redevelop the flow of your ideas on the page.

It is important to make sure that you are always writing up a piece of research. Often this will mean that you need to work on several projects at a time. This should not be a problem, as the experienced researcher realises that many projects do not evolve into full papers worth submitting to high-quality journals.

It can be difficult to find time to write up all of your research ideas and their elaborations during the teaching term, but it is vital that you find the time before those ideas are lost. Given the constraints on our time, it is often a relief when we are able to keep up with the writing up of our ideas. It is good practice, therefore, to ensure that you write for at least 30 minutes per day every day. You should be writing about research that you are exceptionally interested in, so ensure that you view this writing time as a treat and/or a reward for getting other duties out of the way.

However, do not spend so much time writing that it stops you from reading other people's papers and engaging in the discussion of research topics with your colleagues. Reading journal articles and engaging in academic discussion are indispensable as they improve your ability to articulate your understanding of other ideas, and thus save time when you are writing up and contextualising your insightful knowledge.

Research leaders should ensure that their colleagues are able to find time to write and develop their ideas. Sometimes colleagues will lose interest or motivation and become confused about how to develop their ideas. These are key instances where the research leader can step in and make a positive impact, and hence the research leader must learn to read their colleagues' level of engagement and recognise when they need to step in to offer support and guidance during those challenging times.

When a research leader asks their colleagues about their research they are also illustrating that they are interested in their colleagues' work. Research leaders can offer to be a sounding board for something a colleague is mulling over, or inform them that they are very willing to provide feedback on full drafts of their research papers. Sometimes simply asking junior colleagues to write down their ideas in three brief paragraphs can enable them to surmount that mental barrier and reinvigorate their enthusiasm and drive for their research. It is also beneficial for research leaders to encourage colleagues to complete a particular section of a whole paper within a specified time, as this can focus their minds.

When junior colleagues are not finding even small windows of time for their research then their research leader(s) needs to recognise this and try to help them through this drought. Research leaders could lighten the load for colleagues who are finding it difficult to devote time to writing up their research. I have stepped in to present a guest lecture simply to make time for a colleague to complete their paper, and we agreed that in return I would be the first to provide a constructively critical assessment (a pseudo referee report) of their paper by the end of the week. This time-focused agreement, with a degree of reciprocation, focused my colleague's energies to complete their research in draft form. Barriers to the completion of papers can be real or imagined.[1] Research leaders could also help by taking time to talk through any barriers that colleagues are experiencing.

Research leaders need enough capacity in their workload model to enable them to support their colleagues' research endeavours, and they must use this time altruistically. They must approach the person in their faculty whose job it is to arrange their workload and then make a very strong case that it is essential that they have capacity to assist their colleagues effectively and with due care and attention. They must make sure that their manager recognises the immense value of these pastoral efforts. In the words of Jackson (2000, p. 2),[2] "a major difference in the locus of human value is between an instrumental view of people as a means to an end, and a humanistic view of people as an end in themselves." Expressing empathy towards their colleagues about the research challenges they are experiencing[3] can underscore that the research leader is there to provide them with support and that they will draw on their experience to help them fulfil their potential.

NOTES

1. Recent work by Drichoutis and Nayga (2020) suggests that cognitive load has adverse effects on people's performance in reasoning tasks. See Drichoutis, A. C. and Nayga Jnr., R. M. (2020), 'Economic rationality under cognitive load', *Economic Journal*, 130(632), pp. 2382–409.
2. Jackson, T. (2000), 'Instrumental and humanistic values in the management of people: a seven nation study', paper presented at the 11th AGRH conference, Paris, 16–17 November.
3. See Mandadi, T. (2020), '3 ways companies can support grieving colleagues', TED Talk, available at https://www.ted.com/talks/tilak_mandadi_3_ways_companies_can_support_grieving_employees.

3. Drop projects

It is very easy to start a research project with enthusiasm and drive. It is more difficult to realise when a project will not achieve what you expected no matter how much effort you put in. The decision to drop a project is one of the most important decisions you will make as a researcher, simply because it affects the amount of time that you have for other research. As time is scarce, and as we all need to ensure that we produce the best quality research with the greatest impact, we need to be able to step back and realise where our time is best spent. Frequent reflection on which projects to continue and which projects to cease is crucial when you have several running concurrently or very scarce research time.

A good way of reflecting on and realising how much research you are doing is to make a list of those projects. I use an A4 page with six sections, each containing a list of different research projects, as shown in Box 3.1. The page includes submission dates, revision request dates, journal reference numbers, etc. in order to have all the information in one place. Making a list in this way allows you to realise how much time you have for further projects and how thinly you are spreading your research efforts. The list also stimulates reflection on which projects will never be a priority due to their relatively low potential to make a change to the literature and your own competing time pressures. This list will enable you reflect on which papers to discontinue. Note that the sections that you should prioritise are those *under revision* and *polishing*, because those are the papers that are closest to being re/submitted to journals.

BOX 3.1   PRIORITY ORDERING OF RESEARCH OUTPUTS

Revised and Resubmitted:

1. 'Paper name' (co-authors' names) *Journal name* (ABS rank) (names of journals that have already rejected the paper); original submission date 30/09/20; journal ref: XYZ-20-0123; date revision requested: 30/09/20; date revision submitted: 30/11/20.

Under Revision:

2. 'Paper name' (co-authors' names) *Journal name* (ABS rank) (names of journals that have already rejected the paper); original submission date 30/09/20; journal ref: XYZ-20-0123; date revision requested: 30/09/20.

Under Consideration:

3. 'Paper name' (co-authors' names) *Journal name* (ABS rank) (names of journals that have already rejected the paper); original submission date 30/09/20; journal ref: XYZ-20-0123.

Polishing:

4. 'Paper name' (co-authors' names) *Journal target* (ABS rank) (names of journals that have already rejected the paper)

Working On:

5. 'Paper name' (co-authors' names) *Journal target* (ABS rank).

Waiting for Others:

6. 'Paper name' (co-authors' names) *Journal target* (ABS rank).

In Abeyance:

7. 'Paper name' (co-authors' names) *Journal target* (ABS rank).

Books:

A. 'Book name' (co-authors' names) *Publisher* name; target submission date 30/09/21.

Grant Applications:

'Title' (co-authors' names) *Grant funder's name*; deadline for submission 30/02/21.

You will get stuck on projects where progress is slower than you hoped. Sometimes you lose interest in a topic. At other times, you realise that your contribution is not going to be as great as you had hoped. The best thing to do in these circumstances is to put the project in an 'in abeyance' folder and work on something else. If you have low motivation for a project then realise that it is a poor research topic for you, at least at this moment in time.

If you are not making progress, it is likely that you will not have a substantive contribution to make to the literature and hence you will not generate a quality publication. Try not to waste your time – you cannot force insightful thinking! You do not have time to work on everything.

There will be times when you will not be prepared to drop a project as you might have invested so much time and effort into it already; again, put these projects in an 'in abeyance' folder so that you can return to them at a later date if you suddenly have new ideas.

 There will be times when projects appear not to be progressing and other times when your work leaps forward. Be aware that periods of slow progress can be a necessary incubation period before you advance to times of faster progress, and that you cannot force yourself to progress rapidly. Sometimes, no matter what you do, it will feel that you are not making any progress with your research. Park that work, appreciate the journey that it gave you, know that you have learned something from doing it and accept that it is time to move on. It will be there if you ever want to return to it, but make sure that you resist returning to it unless you are sure that you will not be wasting time.

When an idea is clear in your mind then prioritise working on that rather than anything else. Focusing only on one piece of research will enable you to push forward with that research most efficiently. At other times, even when you recognise something is potentially transformative, your mind may need downtime to ensure that you are able to write with the right balance and narrative.

 Research leaders should have a watchful, supportive eye on the progress of their colleagues. They should engage with their colleagues about their research frequently, perhaps even weekly, as although their experience may not be relevant to answer difficult subject-specific questions, they may be able to suggest other ways of thinking about the topic. Sometimes it is simply the act of discussing issues that stimulates a colleague's own thinking and breaks through any thought impediments. If breaking through these barriers is not possible at a point in time, then research leaders should encourage them to write about something that they are able to make progress on.

Research leaders can encourage their colleagues to set themselves targets, such as presenting a research paper by the end of next term. Setting targets can lead to the realisation that you are not identifying anything new, and therefore that piece of research should be placed in an 'in abeyance' folder. If the research project is collaborative between the research leader and a junior colleague, then the research leader should be prepared to step in and cover any duties for a junior colleague if the decision is made that not enough progress has been made. Research leaders and senior co-authors need to reflect on this even more than their junior staff should, since dropping projects with less experienced colleagues can limit the colleagues' development or diminish their confidence. Hence, there may be times when the research leader should continue to co-author a paper with a less experienced colleague even when that research will not meet expectations, as it can provide useful experience for members of their team.

4. Talk, discuss and debate

All of us have different experiences that we draw on, and we should recognise that these experiences are contextualised. An essential part of being a successful academic is to talk with a range of people (including those you agree *and* disagree with in and beyond your department, non-academics, etc.) in order to gain an understanding of others' perspectives, given their experiences, on your research topic. The best way to identify the extent to which you may be correct is to discuss these ideas at every opportunity.

The ideas and comments of knowledgeable peers can lead you to question your assumptions. These remarks from within or outside of your discipline may be critical for the enhancement of your own understanding and could enable you to push your theories forward. Acquire the opinions of the uninformed too in order to give you a reality check and a range of arguments that may question or nuance your innovations.

When you are stuck in your research and find it difficult to move your ideas forward, take the opportunity to talk through your ideas with a trusted mentor. What you need is someone who is both willing to listen and willing to offer you constructively critical comments. That listener might not know the answer or even be able to offer you any useful ideas, but when you try to articulate the problem so that someone else can understand, often you stumble on the answer yourself.

Discuss your research ideas with trusted others whenever you need to, and probably more frequently than that. Present in staff seminars, workshops and conferences as often as you can, whenever you have something to say. Bounce your ideas off colleagues and even your students, to get their opinions and probing questions.

Preparation for a conference speech can provide you with the impetus to organise your ideas in a structure that others can understand. This can make you question what you have done and what you are doing; or possibly steer you in a completely different direction. Use your time preparing for a speech wisely but remember, "We don't see things as they are. We see them as we are" (Anais Nin) and this can cause unconscious bias. We introduce our own interpretation to the issues, and others may not have the same interpretation.

Hopefully, someone at your conference will point out those biases to you in an effort to help.

Research leaders should present a paper in their own staff seminar series at least once a year, not only to show to others that they too are doing some research that has potential flaws, but also to illustrate that they too are on a journey of discovery. When a research leader presents their ideas in an internal seminar, they are not only discussing their topic, they are also illustrating to their colleagues how to present information to other academics and, importantly, how to respond humbly to probing questions.

When colleagues are reticent about participating in departmental opportunities to develop research, they are highlighting that there is a problem. This problem may have something to do with the research environment, the style of questioning or the lack of collegiate atmosphere. It would be beneficial for the research leader to identify whether this is because they do not value such interaction positively or that they are snowed under with other duties. Not valuing the opportunity to debate one's own research with other members of a department will say a lot about the togetherness of a department.

5. Keep presenting

An excellent way to generate feedback on your research is to present your work to others. This can be in staff seminars, impromptu get-togethers, formal conferences or a public talk in a local town hall. You will want to obtain as much feedback on the research topic as possible, so make sure that you formulate your ideas in a way that others can understand by setting the research out clearly and appropriately given the profile and diversity of people's backgrounds within the audience. Be humble and approachable so that others will be willing to give you feedback.

The act of presenting information engenders a structure and flow of material to create an argument. It is only through the iterative cogitation of ideas that this structure and flow are developed and perfected, and this is buttressed and enriched through insightful feedback from others. Undertaking this iterative process on your own may lengthen the process and can keep you going around in circles on particular points. Eliciting opinions on your ideas gives you a reality check and encourages you to question and/or nuance your argument.

Present your research whenever you think you have identified a contribution to the literature. You need feedback, so ensure that others find you approachable and willing to share their criticisms. People are more forthcoming with their feedback if they feel that you will be open to receiving those ideas and that their effort in providing you with feedback will be worthwhile, otherwise they will keep their ideas to themselves.

Offer to present in a staff seminar when you are nearly but not quite ready for feedback, as this can whip you into a frenzy that makes you organise your ideas in a structure that others can understand. This can make you question what you have done and are doing and can steer you in a completely different direction.

You can receive different types of feedback from different seminars, workshops and conferences, as each of these will attract different types of delegate. Some staff seminars enable you to get feedback relatively early in the development of the idea; some workshops provide you with extremely focused comments on small issues; some conferences enable you to showcase the final product. All of these are actively encouraged within context and should be used both with appropriate care and also with gusto and curiosity.

 It is partly the responsibility of a department's research leader to identify relevant conferences and other places to present research ideas for their early career colleagues. One day I was chatting with a junior colleague and realised that they were researching something very interesting and had already published that idea as a paper in our working paper series, but they simply were not ready to present that paper at a conference or submit it to a journal. I knew that their research would be of interest to an acquaintance at another university, so I asked them to look at the working paper and see if it was appropriate for their staff seminar series. I left it up to them about whether they would approach my colleague, but I asked them to assure me that whatever they decided to do they would not mention my initiative. The following day, my junior colleague rushed into my office with the widest grin exclaiming that prof X at university Y had on the off chance seen their working paper and that they were really impressed, and they had invited them to present their work in their staff seminar series. My junior colleague was incredibly excited but did not know whether to accept the invitation. I persuaded them that the worst that could happen is that the audience would find holes in the research that could be subsequently addressed, and hence move the research forward. After some hesitation, they agreed to present in that staff seminar series and the preparation for that presentation accelerated their research. To this day, my colleague is none the wiser about my intervention, and there is no reason why they should be, for these actions should be part of any research leader's efforts to enhance the research quality within the department.

6.   Trial and error

Some researchers try to get things right first time or give the impression that is what they have done; but real research rarely ever works like that. Instead, what we tend to do is define and redefine the problem that we are studying, undertake a type of data collection and test to identify a solution to that problem, learn from the poor results, refine our approach, and try something different until we find a useful solution. Trial and error is sometimes referred to as 'generate and test'; if the test fails to reveal anything useful, then at least you have tried and added to your knowledge that something does not work. Do not be afraid to make mistakes: it is often how the best things are discovered; instead, make sure you learn from mistakes.

I have not failed. I've just found 10,000 ways that don't work. (Thomas Edison)

 We learn and investigate things better when we allow ourselves to make mistakes, and approaching research from a trial and error perspective enables us to progress further with research.[1] Although adoption of this approach can result in a high number of recognisable errors, it also brings you a strong feeling of reward and ever more enjoyment when you discover something substantive. By revising and reflecting on our work we are able to iron out mistakes and learn from oversight. Expect to make many errors or at least for things not to work (!) because you are doing something that no one has done before.

Unfortunately, research assessment exercises do not reward the investigative journey of the researcher, however important and substantive that research may be. Instead, research assessment exercises tend to only recognise research efforts if the researcher finds something that is positive and significant. When your research journey arrives at a dead end, and you realise your research is unlikely to be publishable in a high-quality journal, do not simply confine that research to your file-drawer. Instead, make sure that you learn from the result, reflect on the results, methods, assumptions, associations and interactions, and then realise how you can improve your research further. Transfer that knowledge to the investigation of a connected issue. Your research may not have revealed something timely and substantive to the academic community thus far, but you will have made an important step towards finding out the important issue that required you to have experienced this setback.

Always try to constantly push the boundaries of your research and get your critical friends to help you on this journey. Always debate, recognise your assumptions and realise the crucial and grave limitations in your assumptions and arguments, for it is only by doing so that you will be able to improve your research. Every now and then, you will write something that other people want to hear, so have faith.

Error is the price we pay for progress. (Alfred North Whitehead)

Research leaders must engrain a culture of trial and error within their department, and clearly illustrate to colleagues that failure is part of the journey to success. They should purge the need by fellow researchers to express cagey, protective, defensive behaviours. Effective research leaders use their knowledge to provide guidance to smooth the path to discovery, thereby reducing the extent that errors will be demoralising, enhancing the number of exploratory trials and accelerating their department's rate of research.

The research leader must encourage open debate and knowledge exchange. They should ensure that this is achieved in a mutually respectful culture that nurtures and cultivates the production of ideas while fostering curiosity and intrinsic motivations. A research leader may know very little about the exact area of a colleague's research, but someone else in the department might know something very useful, and this openness and interplay can move the department's core and periphery research activities forward.

Cultivating a culture where trial and error is the expected approach to research requires research leaders to support colleagues when they get things wrong, and make it known that senior colleagues get things wrong too. When a research leader takes the stage in an internal staff seminar and noticeably gets something wrong, then this experience should be understood for the benefit of learning. This proactive innovative and open approach will then be adopted by less experienced colleagues. We are human and fallible, and making mistakes is a natural part of the journey towards improvement. Research leaders can invite adventurous researchers to present their journey of discovery within a staff seminar and ask them to emphasise that they followed a path of trial and error in order to eventually to make a sizeable contribution to knowledge.

NOTE

1. See Harford, T. (2011), *Trial, Error and the God Complex*, TED Talk, available at https://www.ted.com/talks/tim_harford_trial_error_and_the_god_complex.

7.   Do something that really interests you

Enjoy your work and make a change if this does not apply. Although innovations do occur when you are under pressure or experiencing frustrations, under these circumstances it is often the case that these innovations will be rough rather than brilliant diamonds. You can use your frustrations and pressures positively by noting ideas down and exploring them when you are at your inquisitive maximum. You will be at your peak of investigative performance and most imaginative when your brain is enjoying your research. This means that where possible you must be doing something that interests you and not something that is mainly of interest to someone else.

> Pleasure in the job puts perfection in the work. (Aristotle)

Seek answers to questions that really matter to you. If a particular topic does not matter to you, initially or during the journey, then your approach is unlikely to stir the interest of your peers or readership. Feed off your own emotions: they motivate and stimulate you into action, and you can use frustration, annoyance, excitement, purpose, pleasure, astonishment, disgust, courage, joy, happiness and empathy to motivate and succeed in study. Many studies show that higher levels of happiness are associated with higher levels of productivity.[1]

With all the failures that you will inevitably encounter during your research journey, it is paramount that you are passionate about your research topic and this inquisitive drive will power you forward. If you receive rejection letters from journals about your research, then you will retain more energy and drive if your passion for the topic is high, and you can use this enthusiasm to respond to your referees' guidance and improve your own work accordingly. However, when you are bored with a topic, you are less likely to generate the insights and enthusiasm needed to expand your research boundaries and may not elevate your efforts enough to respond positively to their comments.

Ask probing questions to stimulate instrumental and energised controversy. Institutional social scientists recognise that some research activities are undertaken simply to illustrate conformity with a peer group, such as when we implement a method or embrace a particular approach or assume a particular theoretical stance simply because it reflects training or is established in the literature. However, this does not necessarily mean that the method, approach or theoretical stance is the right one to adopt in the specific temporal and physical context that you are investigating. Institutional social scientists also recognise that some research activities will be instrumental, and thus if you find a different method, approach or theoretical stance particularly fascinating, and if there is justification for adopting it, then try it and see where it gets you. Given your intrinsic motivations, it might enable you to reveal something that others have not discovered. Emotions and logic can be mutually supportive, if you can find the right way of combining them. Indeed, writing from the heart can bring the strongest convictions and insights.

If you have control over your research area, avoid doing research because it is expected of you, as you are unlikely to spawn sufficiently insightful ideas, few people will be inspired by your work and it is likely to be a waste of your time.

When you find your research topic to be tedious and dull for a prolonged period, and we all do that temporarily to varying degrees, then actively consider nudging your research in the direction of something that you find more inspiring and interesting. Sometimes, however, you will have to do things that are less interesting for you; in these instances you can choose to (i) change topic, (ii) plough on regardless, or (iii) work with others who are inspired by something that you find boring; team work has many benefits! Be flexible with your use of time; do things that you find inspiring when you can and, when you do not have the inspiration, turn your attention to more mundane activities to clear them.

There will be times when you find everything boring – in which case have a well-earned rest, sit down and read a newspaper, or do something completely different. There will be times when you find everything interesting too, in which case make a priority list and prioritise those things that will have most benefit.

Research leaders should undertake pastoral care activities with their colleagues to ensure that they remain inspired. When anyone realises that a colleague is demoralised about their research, it is the research leader's responsibility to reinvigorate them with supportive, inspiring and enthusiastic insights. This can be hard if you do not know them or the topic well, but that is simply another reason why a research leader should develop excellent interpersonal skills and relationships that enable and support their colleagues' research journeys.

Sometimes a research leader will need to highlight a new method of analysis or remind their colleagues of a different theoretical perspective in order to reinvigorate the research culture. At other times, the research leader will need to encourage inspirational external (potentially collaborative) speakers to present in their staff seminars to add that bit of spark.

NOTE

1. See, for example, Bellet, C. S., De Neve, J.-E. and Ward, G. (2019), 'Does employee happiness have an impact on productivity?' Saïd Business School working paper #2019–13, University of Oxford.

8.   Taking and giving advice

Most academics are supportive, though this varies in intensity and contrasts significantly across departments and institutional cultures. When people shoot your ideas down, try to interpret their criticism in a way that shows your appreciation for their efforts to help you push the idea forward. It is better to realise that an idea does not work earlier rather than later, and you do not want to realise it so late that a journal referee reveals it for you after the long journey to get it to that point. Therefore, make sure that you are able to take critical advice and use it constructively. Help others too by providing them with helpful and constructively critical feedback.

 You will gain respect and become known for helping others if you critically engage with other researchers in a positive and uplifting way. Being consistently positive and uplifting towards others may feel like it saps some of your energy, especially when you are trying to understand differences in opinion and when trying to inform others politely when they are wrong, but it will enable you to grow as a researcher, and this has long-term benefits for you professionally and personally.

Reviewers and colleagues may say that their comments are only minor, but sometimes it is the small things that matter the most. Once you have time to reflect fully on their comments, you may arrive at a completely new level of awareness. The points might seem of little importance at first, but they may be profound and have a huge positive effect on your research achievements over the longer term. The greatest critical friends make comments that have benefits over the long term. Some comments may not be delivered in the most constructive and appropriate manner, and you may feel that you need to lick your wounds, but if your critical friend(s) makes your research better, then this is a good thing, right? Therefore, it is vital that you appear and remain approachable so that others find it easy to give you feedback. Eventually, you will start to recognise yourself getting better and realise the true benefits of those comments, not only in terms of your publication record but also in terms of enhanced satisfaction with your own research, which in turn enhances your own drive to produce more and better research.

Thank all those who give you advice, even when it appears that their comments show a complete lack of understanding of the subject. They gave up their time and energy to think about your research, at least momentarily, and they took the initiative to provide you with those comments in an attempt to help you; it is helpful therefore to at least appear to be grateful. The worst thing that can happen when you pass one of your papers on to a colleague for comments is that they read it and then do not think that it is worth commenting on. If they genuinely think it is worthless, then you should be ready for that criticism and understand why they think that way, as that knowledge will enable you to improve the document. Be open and accessible and make them feel that they can provide you with that feedback. If your own research trajectory starts to level out, it may be because you are not getting enough critical comments from your colleagues. Are others in your department also experiencing that levelling off in their trajectory? Are you content with what you have achieved, or do you want to improve further?

If you try to do everything yourself and do not actively seek constructive feedback, you will be blinkered and not see the obstacles in your way. You may not see the lack of clarity of a point that you are trying to make or the obscurity of a portion of your research, etc. Without advice and feedback, you may not know how to fix a problem or even realise that there is a problem. You need to garner advice and continually muster feedback if you want to continue to improve and achieve your potential.

Never reject advice, even if it is unhelpful, because the next time that person offers you advice, it may be surprisingly useful. Always try to give advice in a visibly constructive manner, but do not be surprised if someone else is not ready to listen to your advice, as they may be distracted and have something else on their mind that is completely unrelated to the advice that you are offering, or alternatively you may have to work on the way that you deliver your critical suggestions. If the timing and phraseology are right, then your comments and feedback to others may not only be opportune, they could also increase the likelihood that they will provide you with useful advice in the future.

It is the full responsibility of the research leader to engender a departmental culture of openness and humility that stimulates the sharing of research efforts, effective communication and feedback. The research leader should be seen to provide useful, constructive and supportive advice to their colleagues, as it will advance the department faster and be a behaviour that others will adopt.

Note that a culture of openness and humility is synonymous with discussion, inter-personal engagement, high levels of interaction and feedback, and very high levels of respect not only for each other's research and achievements, but also for each other as human beings. Respect and civility are mandatory and anything else is unacceptable if the creation of research output is the fundamental departmental objective. If you have no control over this environment and there is no culture of constructive feedback, your research may be best served by leaving the department and joining one with the characteristics that will enable you to thrive.

9. Make time for your research

Duties come your way that you must prioritise, such as teaching and marking. At other times, events in your personal life may prevent you from being able to concentrate fully on a research task. It is important to recognise that there are times when other issues must take priority over your research.

A good habit to try to cultivate is to do a little research every day – make time for your research – as this will conserve your attention on the research issue(s) that you are toiling with most. As solutions to your research problem come into your mind when you least expect it, you need to cogitate about them regularly. The longer you neglect your research topic, the harder it will be to solve that problem and the less chance you will have of making a contribution to the literature.

Pace yourself. If you have this flexibility, do not do too much in one day and try not to time watch. We all need downtime and to be away from our research to recharge our batteries. Lateral thinking is energy draining. Constantly thinking about something in ways that others appear to have never thought about before is mentally exhausting. Hence, make time to do your research often and in short concentrated bursts.

The best research is 'lived'. You must immerse yourself in something in order to understand it fully and recognise how it could be improved. However, only you know how much concentrated time you need for your research, and even then you will not know beforehand whether that time will be a productive success. Can a person simply step into a Formula One car and drive a fastest lap? No, the driver must know and practise the corners, try different racing lines, brake at corners slightly later and generally reflect on what they could do better. All this needs practise and headspace to think differently, and you need to make time to practise. Those who are the most agile and dedicated to their research will, in the end, make the biggest contribution to the literature. Understanding and knowledge are cumulative, and people's abilities improve with practise. Not making regular time available for your research will stunt your progression.

Good researchers allow their research to permeate through their whole life; that does not mean that they allow their research work to interfere with their life, but instead they allow it to complement their life and their identity will reflect it. They discuss their research problem at a coffee shop with a non-academic, which could bore that person or spark great interest; either way, that person may appreciate you discussing your work 'problem' with them, and get the impression that you respect them enough to want to know their views on something. It is surprising what gems of thought some people give you even though they do not know your topic in any depth.

 Research leaders need to identify colleagues who are not achieving their potential and recognise whether this is because they are not making enough time for their research. Help them with time management skills if necessary and encourage them to block out periods of time in their week that they will allocate to research. If they are very stretched with teaching and administrative duties, try to help them to free up some time by making a case for a reduction of this load to those who have increased it. Good research leaders actively search out how to help their colleagues.

10. Know your readership/audience

 I have refereed many papers for journals, and it remains surprising to me how ill-suited some submissions are for particular journals. I also know colleagues who are so desperate to get a paper published in a high-quality journal that they have submitted their papers to journals that are completely inappropriate, and this illustrates the author's lack of knowledge of what the editors and the journal's readers are looking for. It is vital that you know the editorial perspective and readership of a journal prior to the submission of your paper. The same is the case for conference presentations with regard to audience expectations, books with respect to readership and reports with respect to specific stakeholders and external audiences.

 If you misread the interests of an audience or readership then you will be wasting your time and unnecessarily draining your energy. A misread audience can lead to tumultuous discussions that lead to unabridged attacks on ideological foundations, assaults on epistemology and disagreements over world views.

This can happen even when the paper being presented does not explicitly deal with these points and when the presenter is not looking for feedback in those areas.

This can cause you to strongly question what you are doing, why you are doing it and whether it is worth it. The feedback that you receive could be trivial or seemingly irrelevant. If you want to have the feedback that you need then you need to target the right audience and readership.

Once I was invited to present a paper in an external staff seminar but did not put in any effort into knowing who would be in the audience. That paper was a socio-economic geography paper, but one audience member in particular was inflexible and would only approach a research question from a staunchly rational choice perspective. My paper was not designed to question rational choice theory, nor was it designed to justify the use of a socio-economic approach, but that was not how it was taken by a specific audience member and so I spent 90 minutes feeling that I was in front of a firing squad. In hindsight, that was an important learning experience. If I had known the audience would approach a topic in this way, I would have presented a different paper that was built on different assumptions. It was a lost opportunity and a difficult learning experience.

The same issue occurs when submitting papers to journals. Editorial staff will have a particular world view on what represents quality, grounded in a particular ideological, epistemological, methodological or interpretative perspective, and rarely are journals open and flexible enough to entertain significant differences in these areas. You must know who your readership/audience is or your research will not be accepted, and this will create long delays that will postpone the publication of the paper.

 Research leaders should provide advice to their colleagues on where to submit papers and provide guidance on whether the manuscript is even ready for submission. Institutions should ensure that their research leaders have the time and intellectual capacity to read their colleagues' papers and be able to provide them with constructively critical feedback to ensure that the paper is targeted at the right journal with the right readership. A good research leader should know the full range of relevant journals that will be targets for their colleagues' research outputs, as otherwise they will be letting down their team and not providing the support and guidance that their less experienced colleagues require.

PART II

You find inspiration when you least expect it

My experience shows that academics are not machines that can grind out more research when a button is pressed to increase speed. Research requires inspiration and time for reflection and development: your imagination will not be free to innovate and your ideas will not mature without time spent deeply ruminating. Inspirations appear intermittently and reflection is not always productive; for these reasons alone, you should not expect your research to be anything other than sporadically progressive and intermittently effective.

There does seem to be, however, different paths to the achievement of a greater rate of research output, and this section outlines ten ways that appear to work to different extents for different researchers. Discover what works for you by trying other paths that you perceive may benefit you. If an approach did not work for you in the past, it does not necessarily mean that you should dismiss it in the present or in the future. Be agile and responsive to your research needs, which are constantly evolving.

11. Good research is episodic

I never fail to be amazed when a senior colleague expects to publish a new and high-quality research output every academic year. There are very few academics that can simply put pen to paper and expect to produce something good enough to publish in a high-quality journal.

Research is hard, and this difficulty is underestimated by new researchers and naïve line managers. We have other expectations that need completion prior to allocating time to stimulate our research imaginations. Research needs to be prioritised, but researchers need to get other things out of the way to allow them time to do this.

> Start by doing what's necessary, then do what's possible and suddenly you are doing the impossible. (St Francis of Assisi)

 Research is a journey and the experience of good, insightful research is infrequent, unusual and chaotic. Crucially, inspiration comes when you least expect it. There are moments when insightful thoughts bring the answer, that 'Eureka!' moment. There are, of course, many instances when we need time to grind out solutions to a problem by systematically working towards the answer. Wieth and Zachs (2011)[1] found that when people have to solve 'insight problems' that require a high level of creativity, they are much more successful when they tackle these problems at the time of day in which they are least alert. Wieth and Zachs also found that people are more likely to encounter those 'Eureka!' moments when it is their non-optimal working time, i.e. when they do not think their work is most effective. We tend to think that we work best at a particular time of the day, and that is why some of us ensure that we have time to research in the morning while others burn the midnight oil. Hence, Wieth and Zachs assure us that the generation of insightful thoughts typically come to us when we least expect them.

 The main problem with being dependent on something that is episodic is that you do not know when you will get that literature-changing idea. As you do not want to forget it, and as it may well come to you when you are away from your office or even a piece of paper and a pen, then I recommend that you take a notepad or a smartphone with you wherever you go.

Yes, many of our ideas may be hare-brained, and many others will require lots of subsequent development, but if you do not manage to write the idea down when you first receive it, you are likely to forget it.

For some reason, I often get ideas while out on a run over the glorious old Severn Bridge or through the Exmoor countryside. I've had to stop at petrol stations to ask them if I could use their pen and write on a piece of paper, or ask motorists parked by the roadside if I could have a piece of paper to write something down. I have even used dirty water to write a keyword on the inside of my arm to nudge myself to think about a specific thing on my return home. Ideas for some of my best papers have literally woken me up from a deep sleep in the middle of the night and made me turn to a Post-it note pile on my bedside cabinet to write them down.

 I know of academic departments that expect updates of progress on research activities every four months to ensure that you are on track to achieve your academic research targets. The people who set these targets are often those who failed to achieve an academic research record of accomplishment and so entered administration or management instead, and/or are simply following the orders of their superiors in implementing a structure that they perceive generates research output efficiently. Such expectations fail to reflect the reality of the research process and are based on naivety about how research is really carried out. As good research is episodic, setting these goals appears to demoralise active researchers who are attempting to create a big contribution to the literature, suppress a researcher's ability to think laterally, encourage them to make smaller and less substantive contributions to the literature, make researchers question how detached their line managers are from the process of generating quality research output and make active researchers question whether their administrative managers really appreciate the difficulties involved in creating truly innovative research output.

It is essential to recruit the right researchers who are intrinsically motivated to constantly engage in producing research output.[2] Research leaders then need to support their colleagues, feed their minds, inspire them to think in imaginative ways, ask questions that stimulate their brains and give them opportunities to show their thoughts. Research leaders could also ask their fellow researchers for their thoughts on their work, especially as this not only helps the research leader (often in surprising, episodic ways) but also gives the colleague a sense of worth and respect that they can contribute to others' research. Putting pressure on intrinsically motivated colleagues to do high-quality research is likely to have a negative impact.[3]

NOTES

1. Wieth, M. B. and Zachs, R. T. (2011), 'Time of day effects on problem solving: when the non-optimal is optimal', *Thinking and Reasoning*, 17(4), pp. 387–401.
2. Grant (2008) shows that intrinsic motivations strengthen the relationship between prosocial motivation and performance/productivity. See Grant, A. M. (2008), 'Does intrinsic motivation fuel the prosocial fire? Motivational synergy in predicting persistence, performance, and productivity', *Journal of Applied Psychology*, 93(1), pp. 48–58.
3. Ariely et al. (2009) show that many understandings about incentives are wrong and that some extrinsic incentives have the reverse effect on productivity as they *reduce* effort. They show that financial (i.e. extrinsic) incentives *decrease* an individual's performance, and part of this is because it crowds out professional pride. See Ariely, D., Gneezy, I., Loewenstein, G. and Mazar, N. (2009), 'Large stakes and big mistakes', *Review of Economic Studies*, 76, pp. 451–69.

12. Research regularly, but don't work yourself into the ground

Great ideas often come to us when we are relaxed enough to generate those ideas and calm enough to recognise when an idea is a good one. When we work too hard, it is possible to do the mundane well but rarely are we able to produce the exceptional.

 Good research is the result of insightfulness, effort, reflection and reassessments. Engaging with research on a regular basis enables us to think about and reconsider the topic; frequently revisiting our research seems to enable our subconscious to cogitate on the topic and to figure out and shape the research in a way that we are not aware of at the time. This frequency of engagement is important because most of us are not able to write a timeless paper out of the blue, but it is those timeless papers that could be game changers for the discipline or a classic piece that many people will refer to in their own research.

Unfortunately, this cogitation, reflection and reassessment takes time, and time is something that many of us do not allow enough of in our research activities. Cogitation and reflection, in particular, cannot be forced; indeed, cogitation seems to be better when we are enjoying and appreciating the research journey rather than when we want something to be done. Although some of us may be obsessed with writing that extra paper and using up every waking hour to achieve this aim, experience shows us that maintaining a good work–life balance enables us to cogitate and reflect on our work more effectively, and to come to those insightful ideas quicker.

An easy way to lose interest in something is to do it too intensively and too frequently. We must immerse ourselves in our research, but when that research topic becomes a chore, so it becomes less interesting; this is the time to reassess the balance and efforts in your life.

 Time needs to be set aside to discuss ideas with colleagues in an open and informal setting. When we work ourselves into the ground it is already too late to adjust our working rhythm. We should stop what we are doing, have some downtime and pick the topic up again when we are reinvigorated.

A good way to avoid burnout is to take regular breaks. Coffee breaks are times when you can have a well-earned pause. These are essential opportunities to breathe, as they also provide an opportunity for you to reflect and realise whether you are going in the right direction with your research. Coffee times are often opportunities to catch up with friends and acquaintances too, but they are also times to share thoughts on what we are working on. Naturally, we go for coffee with friends and colleagues who we get on well with, but sometimes we need those coffee breaks to be with people that we do not always see eye-to-eye with, as they may provide us with ideas and insightful comments that nudge us to reflect on things that we may not do intuitively.

 Research leaders should keep an eye out for the following occurrences with their colleagues: a change in engagement with research activities; a change in the propensity to take breaks; obsession with an issue without open discussion; shutting down and disengagement; a particularly high opinion of an idea that has not been mooted; and a change in job satisfaction. Observation of any of these behaviour changes may necessitate the need for a delicate discussion in which you may need to identify the issues that are causing stress to overwhelm your colleague. They may be placing an unnecessarily high expectation on their own research activities, and this can reduce their enjoyment and imagination, thereby reducing their ability to undertake research effectively.

13. Take frequent breaks (every 45 mins) while doing research

Research by Dan Schwartz at Stanford University[1] shows that taking time to go for a walk can increase performance in a creativity test. Disengaging from and then re-engaging with research activities enables us to focus for a longer period. Working for prolonged stretches of time without stopping may not be the best way for you to reach your optimal rate of productivity.

I work best when I stick to my natural rhythms, which follow paths of intense activity followed by periods of rest, often of varying lengths. Time-tracking app Desktime[2] found that the most productive people work for 52 minutes and then take a break for 17 minutes. Desktime also notes that employees with the highest productivity ratings typically do not work eight-hour shifts.

The secret is definitely not presenteeism in the office, but it is making sure that you work efficiently and effectively when you have the most creativity and trying to nurture and boost the frequency of that creative time.

 Loehr and Schwartz[3] show that humans have an "ultradian rhythm" where we experience ebbs and flows of energy during the day and this affects many things, including brain activity. When energy levels rise then so do our levels of concentration, creativity, emotional resilience, mental stamina and consciousness, which are all important when undertaking research.

However, after an hour or so, these levels begin to decline and the body needs a short period of downtime to recover and reproduce those levels. Part of the reason for this in our research jobs may be because of fatigue, eye strain, upper limb problems (due to excessive use of keyboards) and backache due to poor posture at the computer.

If you find yourself procrastinating after an hour or so, or have difficulty concentrating, then you probably need a rest and recovery break. The best and most efficient academics do not seem to work for longer hours than the rest of us; instead, they appear to be engaged in more intensive and deliberate activities when they do focus in their work time.

 I like to aim for an intensive 50 minutes of work on a small and well-defined achievable task before taking a ten-minute walk around the office building. However, in practice, this can be an intensive 90 or 120 minutes, simply because I get carried away and do not realise how the time has flown by. Productivity levels can remain high for that period, but a clear 20- to 30-minute break is then required, or fatigue begins to sets in.

When this 'work hard/rest' pattern occurs during a research-only day, these cycles can occur five to seven times a day, depending on the length of time taken for lunch, which typically is not long enough.

Breaks can be spent doing a range of things, but they are better doing things known to be therapeutic, such as breathing in fresh air, looking at and appreciating countryside or meditating, rather than catching up with social media or the news. Meditation, in particular, reduces anxiety levels and can enhance your ability to control your emotions, thinking and worrying.

 Research leaders should make themselves regularly available and accessible to their colleagues. Research leaders should expect to be interrupted frequently during a day at the office. A research leader's role is primarily to ensure that their junior colleagues are enabled and to provide guidance on how to solve their research problems.

However, the research leader also has a responsibility to provide pastoral care to ensure that their junior colleagues are not overly stressed and take frequent breaks. A research leader must habitually tour their department[4] and check that their colleagues are taking breaks and not depriving themselves of regular breaks that create space and opportunities to gain insights and ideas.

A research leader should make a point of knowing what their colleagues are interested in, what sports teams they support and generally what's going on in their lives, so that if a colleague looks worn out and stressed they can initiate a conversation that brings the colleague back to reality, perhaps over a coffee or a walk-and-talk around the campus. Importantly, a research leader should also encourage at least one of their colleagues to check on them every now and then, because frequent interruptions by junior staff can stifle progress in their own research and add to their own stress level; research leaders also need to take regular breaks!

NOTES

1. See https://news.stanford.edu/news/2014/april/walking-vs-sitting-042414.html.
2. See http://www.desktime.com.
3. Loehr, J. and T. Schwartz (2005), *The Power of Full Engagement*, Simon and Schuster.
4. Dewey argues that habits of action are flexible responses that are adaptable to unique situations, rather than mechanical responses with a given outcome. See Dewey, J. (1922/2012), *Human Nature and Conduct*, Digireads.

14. Exercise

Participate in regular exercise that gets your heart rate up. Exercise enhances your ability to focus and can give you an immediate improvement in your mood due to the release of serotonin. Due to lower anxiety levels, your focus will improve and be sustained over a longer period.

 Wendy Suzuki, a Professor of Neural Science and Psychology in the Center for Neural Science at New York University, argues that exercise is the most transformative thing that you can do for your brain. This is because (i) it has immediate effects on your brain; a single workout that you do will immediately increase levels of neurotransmitters (such as dopamine, serotonin and noradrenalin) that increase your mood right after your workout, (ii) a single workout can improve your ability to shift and/or focus attention, and that improvement will last for at least two hours, and (iii) studies have shown that a single workout will improve your reaction times.[1] She continues to argue that short-term benefits that immediately follow exercise can have much longer benefits because exercise actually changes brain anatomy, physiology and function. She contends that exercise increases the number of brain cells and increases the brain's volume and long-term memory, improves attention function, and enhances long-term mood.

 Do exercise whenever you can. I find it best to integrate exercise into my daily schedule: walk to work or take a 20-minute downtime at lunchtime by walking around the campus. Walk upstairs instead of taking the lift. Walk to the shops instead of taking the car. You tend to get the best ideas *not* when you are focused and working hard on a particular problem but instead when your brain is relaxed. My ideas often come to me when I am on an evening's run through the countryside in the fresh air surrounded by relaxing views that uplift my mood and seemingly stimulate my subconscious to fix those long-standing unsolved research riddles. Walk-and-talk meetings with an informed and interested colleague can have similar effects.

 There is a growing literature highlighting that exercise is linked with brain development. Encourage your colleagues to participate in more physical activities by, for instance, organising a lunchtime walk around the campus with your colleagues, a staff squash league or a staff five-a-side football team, but be mindful of including all colleagues.

One of my previous universities encouraged physical exercise, and particularly so during the month of February. Every year they ran a pedometer challenge and every year we entered a team from within my department. We never won, but that was not important, as it was the taking part that mattered. During this competition, there seemed to be a need to walk that little bit further to try to contribute to the team's overall step count. One year the university changed the standard step count system and instead requested step counts over a two-week period, with the first week being the establishment of a baseline set of data and the second week being the actual number of step counts. Interestingly, everyone in our team increased the number of steps during the second week relative to the baseline week, perhaps because they not only wanted to contribute to the team's overall count but also because they wanted to ensure that they experienced an increase in the number of their own steps that week. Now, I can't be sure that there was an increase in long-term exercise or that the overall focus of the team members went up, but we did feel slightly closer as a group, which had important benefits.

NOTE

1. See   https://www.ted.com/talks/wendy_suzuki_the_brain_changing_benefits_of _exercise?language=en.

15. Know your own strengths in collaborative research

Collaborative research can be easier or more difficult than working on your own. It is not unusual for your presentation at a conference to be followed by a coffee with someone who has been inspired by your presentation. Take heart that this is a good thing, and when they suggest writing a follow-up paper together that marries your and their ideas this can be a fruitful and effective way to accelerate your research and to explore unexpected tangents. Whether you decide to collaborate with them or not should be based on an informed judgement rather than an automatic reaction to a complementary and enjoyable post-presentation conversation.

Consider whether you will be able to make an important contribution to that research, how much time it will take you away from other research with varying priorities, the qualities and abilities of the potential collaborator, and how much you expect to learn and how that knowledge will help you in the future. Network building is good, but those networks and relationships need to work productively, and this will depend on which of your strengths you are bringing to a team, as well as their strengths.

Collaborative activities can be a good or a bad distraction from your own research activities. It is favourable to help less experienced colleagues or to assist others in their research – and this type of scholarly activity will foster a positive reputation – but collaborating on projects that are too tangential to your own research area(s), or that are an inefficient use of your time and effort, could set you back. Collaborating can enable you to expand your network and become better known for your research prowess. It is a helpful opportunity for you to reflect on your own areas of strength; but a downside is that, inevitably, you will also be known for your areas of weakness. If you are collaborating with a positive crowd, they will appreciate your strengths and you will collectively work together to build on each other's strengths and cover each other's weaknesses. This does mean that you need to know your own strengths and contribute to research teams based on those strengths.

Make sure that you have the opportunity to grow in any collaborative research and ensure that you can make an important contribution that will build on your own areas of strength; if neither of these is the case then seriously consider turning down the offer to collaborate. There will be many other opportunities for collaboration, especially if you come across at conferences as an approachable, clever, clear and positive researcher.

A problem can arise when you work with people who expect you to do all the work for them. If your collaborators are simply contracting out the work that they should be doing – perhaps they rationalise this in a way that they are encouraging less experienced staff or saving their own precious time – then you are likely to remain inferior in their minds. The only things they will recognise is whether you did the work correctly, on time and without any fuss: if it took you longer than it should due to you undertaking work out of your area, then their perception of you may deteriorate. I suggest that you set out clear responsibilities for each individual at the outset and avoid collaborating with academics who simply want to save their own time and effort.

Alternatively, you could use these opportunities to learn from the best. They may take the opportunity to show you new techniques, different perspectives, an alternative framework or something else that could benefit you in the longer term. Essentially, be reflective on the opportunities for collaboration as they come your way, because they may not always bring the benefit that you may anticipate.

 If you know that one of your colleagues is simply being used in a non-beneficial way, and if you consider this to be a poor experience for them, then proactively support them by highlighting other work and relationships that would be more advantageous for them.

On the other hand, do actively encourage your colleagues to participate in collaborative activities, as it can expand their skills, networks, perspectives and knowledge, which will help their career development and reflect well on your department.

Research leaders should actively seek collaborative research activities for their colleagues. They could promote their colleagues' skills across their own networks to encourage knowledge sharing and integration across academia. Research leaders could show the benefits of collaboration through clear examples, such as by emphasising the benefits of writing in collaboration with colleagues within their department. Research leaders will have to nurture their colleagues for part of this learning process, but it will enable their colleagues to grow in ways that they and the department should benefit from.

16. Asking unusual questions permits us to detect unusual things

Having the audacity to ask unusual questions permits you to generate unusually interesting answers. The presence of unusual things in your research makes your research distinctive, and this distinctiveness enhances the likelihood that your research is accepted for publication.

 Every academic probably feels mimetic pressures to conform to a mainstream view. Instead of envisaging these pressures as a competition between a mainstream and a heterodox alternative, try to see contrasting perspectives as interdependent with interacting, competing relations that encourage the generation of novel ideas through the exercise of contrasting powers. After all, whether something is mainstream is socially and ideologically determined. Question everything. Always ask the 'so what?' question, as doing so may mean that you arrive at the conclusion that something is trivial.

Daydreaming is an important component in the imagination process. Daydreaming empowers us to think laterally, and it is acknowledged that daydreaming is constructive in many contexts.[1] Research by Vinod Menon suggests that daydreaming is good for us and that

> Mental downtime engages ... (the problem-solving) brain system, allowing us to think about problems differently without a sense of urgency, linking different thoughts that we might otherwise not have, reflect on our thoughts and actions, and internalise memorable events in ways that enrich our inner lives.[2]

Mental downtime (including sleep and daydreaming) is necessary and is proven to be a way to engage with more insightful innovations; it allows us to stumble over unusual questions that may not have been realised when we have high levels of focus and attention. For instance, Home (1988)[3] found that sleep-deprived individuals were less creative, Walker (2009)[4] found that sleep enhances relational connections and Wagner et al. (2004)[5] found that greater sleep enabled more insightful thoughts. Walker et al. (2002)[6] found that when participants in their study were woken from sleep when they were experiencing rapid eye movement, they performed better at solving a problem, and it is widely recognised that rapid eye movement is when you have fluid reasoning and flexible thought.

We also know that longer sleeping times are associated with higher wages (Biddle and Hamermesh, 1989)[7] in the labour market, although the causality here is debatable. One paper that has tried to solve that causality problem is by Gibson and Shrader (2018),[8] who find that a one-hour increase in location-average weekly sleep increases earnings by 1.1 per cent in the short run and by 5 per cent in the long run. It remains unconfirmed whether Gibson and Shrader's result is because greater sleep makes people more agreeable and less irritable, or whether greater sleep enhances lateral thinking and an improvement in our ability to solve problems.

So, whenever you have the chance, catch up on that well-earned sleep, relax and let your mind wonder. You will be consciously and purposefully investing in your imagination and knowledge generation. Do recognise that you need more downtime when you are working your hardest; that downtime might even help you solve that problem that you've been cogitating about. Instead of working late, take a break.

Research leaders need to make sure that their colleagues are not burning themselves out and avoiding downtime. This is mandatory for the generation of ideas over the long term and to ensure a high level of well-being for your colleagues. There will always be some colleagues who constantly push themselves forward to achieve more, and this is both admirable and commendable, but there is also a tipping point after which this can have a negative effect on an individual's health. You should want your colleagues to ask unusual questions, have the freedom to ask these questions in non-standard ways, and this often requires them to have downtime to engage in those daydreaming activities.

If a research leader catches a colleague daydreaming, they should congratulate them for taking the opportunity and encourage them to have the confidence to share those wondering research-related thoughts. Research leaders should also daydream at work, and visibly so, in order to demonstrate to your colleagues that this is perfectly acceptable and is actually a symbol of imaginative thinking.

NOTES

1.   Tierney, J. (2010), 'Discovering the virtues of a wandering mind', *New York Times*, published June 28th.
2.   See   https://news.stanford.edu/thedish/2014/09/30/stanford-psychiatrist-tells-us -why-it-is-good-to-daydream/.
3.   Home, J. A. (1988), '"Sleep loss" and "divergent" thinking ability', *Sleep: Journal of Sleep Research & Sleep Medicine*, 11(6), pp. 528–36.

4. Walker, M. P. (2009), 'The role of sleep in cognition and emotion', *Annals of the New York Academy of Sciences*, 1156, pp. 181–3.
5. Wagner, U., Gals, S., Halder, H., Verleger, R. and Born, J. (2004), 'Sleep inspires insight', *Nature*, 427(6972), pp. 352–5.
6. Walker, P., Liston, C., Allan Hobson, J. and Stickgold, R. (2002), 'Cognitive flexibility across the sleep–wake cycle: REM-sleep enhancement of anagram problem solving', *Cognitive Brain Research*, 14, pp. 317–24.
7. Biddle, J. E. and Hamermesh, D. S. (1989), 'Sleep and the allocation of time', NBER paper 2988.
8. Gibson, M. and Shrader, J. (2018), 'Time use and labor productivity: the returns to sleep', *Review of Economics and Statistics*, 100(5), pp. 783–98.

17. Read, write, reread and rewrite

Research is a journey of discovery that twists and turns, with episodes of great accomplishment and realisation, and other instances that seem like dead ends. The act of writing and redrafting enables you to enhance the clarity of your arguments and helps you to reflect on and reassess the links that you have made between points. Redrafting text also enables you to reconsider these issues in more depth and perhaps even from a slightly different context, thereby enabling you to generate more ideas and reflections, especially on the connections between points.

 Writing articles for journal publication requires an iterative process that not only mandates the redrafting of your own text, but also the rereading of others' texts in light of your updated way of understanding issues. We do not fully understand the full ramifications of our ideas when those ideas are in their infancy and, because of this, we may not make links between our own and others' research. We need to pick up, put down, flick forward and flick backwards in our reading of texts, especially books, and this reflection is time intensive. Unfortunately, the flicking forward and backwards in timeless texts can be effectively discouraged by e-versions of texts when their reading licence constrains our ability to read more than, say, 30 pages or a chapter at any point in time.

Research questions can evolve. New ways of phrasing and thinking about relationships between variables spring to mind, and then they need to be established as reproductions of pre-existing ideas or new and novel contributions. All this takes time to develop and to cross-reference with the existing literature, but is an essential thing to do. Rereading and rewriting texts makes arguments more succinct, more developed, more meaningful and more fluent.

Part of this circular process of research, including estimating and re-estimating results, can come under the category of HARKing, which is where we construct a Hypothesis After a Result is Known (Kerr, 1998).[1] Rubin (2017)[2] provides a nuanced discussion about when HARKing is likely to be bad for science, and Hollenbeck and Wright (2016)[3] suggest this can take two forms (SHARKing, which is Secretly HARKing, and THARKing, which is Transparantly HARKing), where THARKing is arguably justifiable in its place.

Given the dominance of iterative secondary data analyses within many social sciences, it would be difficult to rule out categorically the possibility of HARKing from many published papers. Even if we generate results that we choose not to revisit and revise, readers will nuance their interpretation of our results due to their experiences, further reading, reflection, perspectives of confounding issues, etc. We need to write and rewrite our texts to moderate and rein in our over-interpretation of our results, but we also need to do this to strengthen our ideas and recognise their relevance in different contexts.

 When we first collate our data and are satisfied that we have generated the database ready for analysis, it is often too easy to draw conclusions with an excessive degree of confidence. Exercise caution and ensure that you do not get carried away with initial results, since they may simply be confirming someone else's results that you have not read yet or that you chose to ignore because you did not expect your analysis to venture down that route.

Deciding when a paper is ready for feedback and then ready for journal submission is always difficult. If the paper is submitted to a journal too soon with results that are not as novel as you claim (perhaps with the referee informing you that someone else has already trodden those paths), then you should have waited and thoroughly reviewed and reread the literature in order to reflect on and identify the true value of your research. On the other hand, if you delay submitting a paper that has some very new, temporally relevant findings, you are missing the crest of a wave. It is difficult to time this correctly, and you should always ask a trusted colleague with similar research interests to advise you on this.

It is vital to rewrite your text and weave into your arguments the contemporarily relevant ideas, especially as your referees will expect you also to be at the frontier of knowledge in the area. Weaving that knowledge into your text allows you to create new knowledge, new connections and new contributions to the literature.

 A research leader should be available to provide advice and guidance on when and whether a paper is ready for submission to a journal. They should emphasise the importance of this timeliness and they can illustrate this by asking the less experienced staff for similar advice (perhaps at the same time as asking one of their usual trusted advisors). By following this process, a research leader is able to strengthen collegiality in the department.

If the research leader knows the colleagues' literature particularly well, they should also be able to bring new literature to the attention of colleagues, or they could ask a colleague in another university to provide feedback to a junior colleague.

It is good practice for a research leader to ensure that new literature is continually being brought to the attention of junior and senior colleagues. This is easy to do, simply by forwarding on emails containing the contents of new issues of journals, especially those journals that they may not pay particular attention to. Such a simple and mindful process strengthens the impression that the research leader is there to support and help their junior colleagues.

NOTES

1. Kerr, N. L. (1998), 'HARKing: hypothesising after the results are known', *Personality and Social Psychology Review*, 2(3), pp. 196–217.
2. Rubin, M. (2017), 'When does HARKing hurt? Identifying when different types of undisclosed post hoc hypothesising harms scientific progress', *Review of General Psychology*, 21(4), pp. 308–20.
3. Hollenbeck, J. R. and Wright, P. M. (2016), 'Harking, Sharking and Tharking: making the case for post hoc analysis of scientific data', *Journal of Management*, 43(1), pp. 5–18.

18. Thrive on lots of different experiences

Variety is the spice of life. Our own idiosyncratic experiences stimulate us to make distinctly different connections between potentially connected issues. People following a similar life path are likely to make similar connections, but it is sometimes our different evolutionary paths that matter when shifting the literature forward.

Embracing variety, encountering new experiences and taking the time to reflect on new knowledge can all affect the way that we do our research and can influence the way that we interpret, accept and integrate new knowledge into our research. A diversity of experiences can also enable us to question things from a slightly different angle from the norm, and this is incredibly valuable and useful when attempting to reinterpret and enhance our collective understanding of information. Get out of your comfort zone!

 Remaining in your comfort zone can provide you with a sense of safety and security, but it can also make you and your research more predictable and less likely to contribute something distinct to the literature. Your comfort zone can limit your breadth of responsiveness to opportunities, stop you from challenging yourself and your ideas, and confine you to a furrow where you are unresponsive to real-world challenges.

However, too much discomfort (such as public speaking, media engagement or teaching your topic as a service module in a different discipline) can be dreadful. Skydiving can challenge your fears and make you realise that what is holding you back is often yourself, sometimes in response to your experiences but sometimes in response to social norms (both of which may be out of context and inappropriate to hold you back in the present). Do not let your fears and biases get in the way; instead, try to unpick those expectations and realise the most in those opportunities. In this way you will learn to circumnavigate your own self-imposed limitations.[1]

 Take every opportunity to experience different contexts, gather different understandings and garner and appreciate perspectives that challenge your own. Thrive on lots of distinctly different experiences and actively search for them, as they will strengthen your understandings of a variety of social issues and even shift your own understandings forward.

Purposefully take yourself to a different place to write up your research. A week in Spain or the Lake District, or somewhere else that you find inspirational, can refresh your reflective writing style and embolden you to write up your research in an inspiring way.

Present your research to other academics in a challenging and different environment, as you may be surprised by their questions and your ability to respond in an agile manner. Take notes of the different angles of questioning in those different environments to ensure that you are cognisant of the different possible ways that your referees may regard your work.

 Research leaders should showcase their ability to get out of their own comfort zone and emphasise that this is encouraged to accelerate academic progress. Being in an environment that is challenging as well as supportive stimulates faster knowledge creation and innovative research. Ask colleagues at other universities to attend your own staff seminar series when they would be interested in the topic of an internal presenter. Encourage them to ask (nicely and constructively critically) probing questions that accentuate their interest in the presenter's topic (especially when the presenter is a junior staff member) and challenge the presentation in the hope of moving their research forward.

In an inspiring TED Talk, Patrice Gordon (2020) argues that there is a need for reverse mentoring as senior colleagues often have blind spots and biases.[2] Less experienced researchers informally mentoring more senior staff provides those junior staff members with greater ownership and sense of worth, but it is much more than this because it also heightens the humanistic (rather than functional) tendencies within your research cluster. Gordon argues that if senior staff recognise and understand different perspectives, often brought to their attention by engaged junior staff, they become more inclusive and better leaders. Although there may be a need to formalise these reverse mentoring opportunities, the best leaders are already open and accessible to junior staff and very much welcome such inspiring interactions. The sharing of these different experiences and perspectives can broaden colleagues' understandings and horizons across all levels of seniority.

NOTES

1.   Raglin and Turner (1993) emphasise the benefits of a being in the zone of optimal functionality for sportspeople, and Keeley et al. (2008) find a similar zone for undergraduate students. See Raglin, J. S. and Turner, P. E. (1993), 'Anxiety and performance in track and field athletics: a comparison of the inverted-U hypothesis with zone of optimal function theory', *Personality and Individual Differences*, 14(1), pp. 163–71; Keeley, J., Zayac, R. and Correia, C. (2008), 'Curvilinear relationships between statistics anxiety and performance among undergraduate

students: evidence for optimal anxiety', *Statistics Education Research Journal*, 7(1), pp. 4–15.
2. See https://www.ted.com/talks/patrice_gordon_how_reverse_mentorship_can _help_create_better_leaders ?language=en.

19. Polishing papers properly takes a long time

All papers should have the right balance between the big picture and details, but this perception of balance will vary across journals, referees, editors and readerships, and it can make the difference between acceptance and rejection. An academic paper should make a very clear argument, and it should be convincing. The easier the paper is to read and understand, the more likely it will be accepted for publication, as poorly written papers almost always command less complimentary referee reports. However, the clarity of the paper is associated with the rate of the flow of ideas, and what may appear clear to one person may appear unclear to another.

 The balance between the big picture and details is a difficult one to achieve. Try to exclude particulars that detract from the principal research area but include specifics that are interesting and show your depth/breadth of knowledge.

In my experience, the two most important sections of any paper are the abstract and the introduction. If the abstract does not catch the editor's attention, then you are already on the path to receive a desk rejection. If the introduction is not strong, does not emphasise the contributions of the paper or does not underline its substantive importance to the literature, then you will lose the referees' enthusiasm and goodwill even before the paper is read fully. Make sure that your paper is crystal clear about why your content and flow of ideas are both new and important.

 Ask people with plenty of publication experience to read and comment on the 'readiness' of your paper for journal submission. You will always save time by obtaining useful and critical feedback from your colleagues and incorporating it into the paper, because it increases the chance that the paper will be strong enough and enhances the likelihood that the substantive argument contained within the paper comes shining through to the reader. If your colleagues do not understand something or think something is not clear enough to them, or if they would prefer examples to support a particular point, then it is likely that a referee is going to think the same.

Polishing papers properly takes a huge amount of time because you need to question whether your contribution will be understood by people with varying perspectives. It also requires you to second-guess why referees may reject the paper, so that you can eliminate those issues before the referee has the chance to state those concerns. Often it is the organisation and flow of the ideas that are important, rather than simply the content. If you find this difficult, try to factor in a four-week gap between the completion of a full draft and when you polish the document. Stepping away from the paper allows you to reflect critically on the script with a fresher pair of eyes, and it can result in a modest redrafting of the script that more eloquently expresses your ideas.

One important aspect of the paper is the flow of the argument. Always put tangential comments, however interesting they may be, in a footnote or endnote (depending on the journal's style) to ensure a smooth transition between subsequent points. The argument must be straightforward and should not meander.

 Research leaders will have a wealth of experience writing journal articles. They should impart their publishing experience to their colleagues and consistently offer to read and provide feedback on their colleagues' articles. Often, junior colleagues do not recognise the huge amount of effort that is needed to polish papers effectively, the different ways that readers interpret sentences and the need to ensure clarity of argument throughout a paper. Of course, the longer the manuscript, the more difficult this is to do. Research leaders should edit working or discussion paper series and act as a gatekeeper to ensure quality, clarity and succinctness in colleagues' research outputs. Encouraging submission to a working/discussion paper series and providing a fast (maximum ten days) turnaround is good practice, and reduces the probability of colleagues receiving journal desk rejection letters and the associated reduction in morale this may engender.

20. Learn to have time away from research

When I visit different departments, I am often surprised by how many office doors are shut and by the lack of interaction between staff members. I am also surprised by the pace at which some people are working, relentlessly exceeding contract hours. We all have uncomfortable and inconvenient deadlines, and many of us have extensive teaching requirements. However, it is vital to give your brain a rest from striving to achieve specific tasks. You must give your brain downtime. Not only does over-working increase the likelihood that you will burn out, it also makes you less interesting and more disconnected from reality. Not having downtime is detrimental to you personally and professionally.

Downtime is necessary to rejuvenate your intrinsic motivations, to avoid burnout and to revive your mojo. Time away from your work can be thought of as essential maintenance for your psyche and it allows your body to recover from the stresses and strains of your mental agility. Downtime, and daydreaming more specifically, has been shown to be necessary to enhance our ability to think imaginatively. Manoush Zomorodi (2017)[1] recalls a conversation with Dr Sandi Mann who conducted a number of experiments with humans and provided evidence that people who have downtime and get bored then think more creatively than those who do not have downtime and never experience being bored.

All work and no play make Jack a dull boy. (Proverb)

Integrate regular bouts of time away from your work into your research schedule, with a frequency that you need to ensure that you retain your intrinsic motivations to do your research and retain a wellspring of ideas. When you start to notice that you are making too many frustrating errors, or when you are generating very few creative ideas, that is also a time to take a break. You will work more productively and effectively when your brain has had a chance to clear and settle. Returning to your research problem after a period of rejuvenation will enhance your accuracy and focus, and allow you to solve your research problem more quickly.

 A research leader should set precedents by encouraging departmental participation in collegiate extra-work activities. These should be on various days and times so that all have a chance to engage, e.g. parental duties will stop researchers with families from engaging in activities after, say, 3 p.m. One suggestion is a departmental coffee break, especially if you have a staff room.

I had a head of department who informally called by my office to see how I was doing every Friday afternoon. These seemingly ad hoc conversations started with a friendly and inquisitive "So, what research are you working on today?" but soon shifted to "Are you doing anything interesting at the weekend?" Simply engaging with each other in a social and non-work-related way – without being intrusive – can bring a much-needed reality check into the workplace, especially when your research at that time is particularly abstract.

NOTE

1. Zomorodi, M. (2017), *Bored and Brilliant*, St. Martin's Press.

PART III

Broaden your methodological toolbox

It is a disappointing reflection of society when a group like the exceptionally prestigious American Economic Association (AEA)[1] has to remind its members of best practices for diversifying research. The AEA needed to remind economists of the need to "read and cite diversely" and to "think inclusively" not least by "finding value in alternative research approaches" to "improve your research and the discipline". Bruce Caldwell (1989, p. 44) famously wrote:

> Methodological pronouncements are usually only roughly thought out: they contain seemingly random citations of sometimes incompatible philosophical positions; there is usually an implicit political agenda which is carefully hidden by a veneer of scientific objectivity; almost always the point is to direct the reader to embrace a particular theory; and there is often a specific opponent in mind as well as fellow travellers, but they are seldom explicitly identified.[2]

There is snobbery present in some social science disciplines, especially with the selection of research methods, and this has been the case for decades. Part of the reason for this pomposity is the need for authors within a discipline to follow methodological expectations and conform to their narrow methodological training. Some universities teach only quantitative methods in some of their social science disciplines! Increasing the breadth of research methods training at under- and postgraduate levels would rectify this problem.

We can apply a wide range of research methods in our social science research, and the method that we should select is the one that is most appropriate for the research question; however, this research method is not necessarily the one that conforms to a discipline's methodological expectations. Rephrasing a research question so that you can answer it with a single method is no excuse for a lack of awareness of the strengths of other methods and a lack of awareness of the limitations of applying your discipline's preferred methodological approach. Effective advancement of knowledge requires agility in the use of research methods and their appropriate applications.

NOTES

1. See https://www.aeaweb.org/resources/best-practices.
2. Caldwell, B. J. (1989), 'Post-Keynesian methodology: an assessment', *Review of Political Economy*, 1(1), pp. 43–64.

21. Econometrics

The vast collection of secondary quantitative data permits many searches for a line through a plot of that data and the identification of a clear statistical relationship. Effective knowledge of econometrics provides the researcher with a remarkably useful tool that can be used to identify patterns in numbers that can then be interpreted to support particular theories.

Although there are many developments in the applications of econometrics and the approach is effective if drawing lines through a scatter of points,[1] econometrics is only one of many research methods that can be applied to identify an answer to a research question. Reliance on only one method of analysis can be at the cost of wider exploration and knowledge accumulation which could be achieved through the application of a triangulation of research methods.

Econometrics is arguably the most useful way to identify patterns in strings of numbers. Exploratory analyses of strings of numbers can reveal statistical relationships that we did not know existed, whereas confirmatory analyses of quantitative data can enable us to claim with a particular level of statistical confidence that a relationship did not occur by chance.

However, this should not mean that econometric approaches are without criticism. Strong critics of the potential over- and misuse of econometrics include Ziliak and McCloskey (2008, p. 2).[2] These authors go as far to state that reducing social science and economic problems to testing, estimation and interpretation with the reliance solely on statistical significance is an extremely bad idea and is "causing a loss of jobs, justice, profit and even life" because it is "neither necessary nor sufficient for proving discovery of a scientific or commercially relevant result". They argue that "Statistical significance should be only a tiny part of an inquiry concerned with the size and importance of relationships."

There is a multitude of ways to estimate econometric models, including continuous variables (e.g. 32.456356), dichotomous (e.g. yes/no), categorical (e.g. a Likert scale: strongly agree, agree, neither agree nor disagree, disagree, strongly disagree) and fractional (e.g. 42 per cent of an electorate voted for a particular political party in a general election) data. You can test for statistical correlations where there are time lags and time leads (e.g. house prices affect home rental values a year later). You could explore trajectory patterns over time, such as the development of one idea relative to other ideas. The range of econometric applications to most types of data is seemingly infinite.

Given that part of my training was in econometrics, it is probably inevitable that I would push for at least the partial use of econometric methods for the analysis of quantitative data relating to many research problems. I often use this research method to set the scene and identify unusual observations (or outliers) that can be the focus of follow-up qualitative investigations. Application of a triangulation of research methods is preferable, however, as a result is often sensitive to the research methods used.

 Research leaders should either know how to assist and guide less experienced researchers through the applications of econometrics or they should know where such assistance and guidance can be sourced. I often pick the brains of a gentleman and scholar of statistics who provides me with unwavering support and guidance. Research leaders should provide feedback on research matters to their colleagues on a regular basis, and they should ask their colleagues for views on their econometric work too, as this generates a reciprocal, mutually respectful, constructively critical, working relationship.

NOTES

1. Many within the economics discipline see use of econometrics as a prerequisite to enter the profession and expect that a lot of time is spent during an economist's career improving their knowledge of the approach.
2. Ziliak, S. T. and McCloskey, D. N. (2008), *The Cult of Statistical Significance*, University of Michigan Press. See also McCloskey, D. and Ziliak, S. T. (1996), 'The standard error of regressions', *Journal of Economic Literature*, 34, pp. 97–114.

22. Statistics

Statistical methods come in many shapes and forms and, typically, they allow us to gain an aggregate understanding of data. Different statistical methods enable us to gain a variety of insights into the data, and although an accomplished statistician may prefer to apply a particular type of statistical method to data, they will acquire an arsenal of statistical approaches and a whole battery of tests to enable them to explore the data flexibly and effectively.

Statistical methods are not usually designed to reveal specifics about individual units in a data set, and hence they are not designed to provide in-depth understanding or to reveal the *whys*. Instead, they can be perfect to reveal a range of potentially very useful *whats*.

Statistics allow us to infer something about a population and to draw generalisations. These can be especially useful when setting the scene for a deeper analysis, perhaps using qualitative methods to reveal the whys. Statistical findings can be useful to infer something universal in a data set too, and they really should be the bread and butter of any social science exploration because they can be very helpful to establish and describe, at the very least, the statistical context of the research.

But don't get dogmatic about statistics: they are there to provide us with generalities and to inform us about some average or pattern that is present in the data. The real value of statistical analysis comes from the careful modelling and interpretation of this data, clarity on the limitations of the modelling approach and data availability, and in the recognition and appreciation that the statistical results can have a variety of interpretations that can be associated with a set of different theories.

Econometric research methods are very useful when finding evidence to support a variety of theoretical models. On the other hand, statistics are particularly useful for the mathematical analysis of statistical models and for the presentation of data. Statistics can provide strong guidance on sampling, weighting and bias when we are collecting and understanding data, which includes both averages and, often more importantly, the variation in the sample.

If your research question can be stated in a way that a number would be an appropriate answer, then statistics are an essential part of your research methods toolkit. A flexible social science researcher will use a range of methodological approaches that are most appropriate for the investigation of a particular research topic. Full knowledge of the whole range of statistical methods is probably not possible for a social science researcher, so instead the social science researcher should know how to identify the correct statistical method when it is needed, and then have the ability to self-train and apply that method. Different situations require different statistical approaches, so applying the same method whatever the circumstances is likely to generate a suboptimal set of answers.

 One role of the research leader is to assist in the identification of appropriate statistical methods and to be a sounding board in identifying answers to a research question. When research leaders read and provide feedback on colleagues' manuscripts, they should have a focus on identifying areas of potential dispute that journal referees may identify. Research leaders should highlight gaps in manuscripts that could be filled with the application of extra statistical tests and be able to describe how a method could strengthen the argument. Regular chats or reviews of colleagues' research outputs can enable the suggestion of alternative and potentially more fruitful statistical approaches earlier in the research journey.

23. Questionnaires

Underlying many statistical analyses are data collected via questionnaires. Even national GDP figures have firm-level questionnaire survey data at their core, and there will inevitably be at least an element of bias when collecting any data. Given your specific research question, a correctly worded questionnaire will provide you with more appropriate data than using someone else's secondary data, and hence it is more likely that you will be able to contribute to the literature, so collect your own data using a questionnaire! Generating your own questionnaire can be extremely valuable and could be the only way for you to have appropriately worded questions and therefore the answers to your innovative research questions.

 Secondary data sets collected by someone else or by some other organisation were most probably not collected for answering your specific research question. Questionnaires were designed to answer a research question that was theoretically appropriate at or prior to the time when the data were collected. Time has moved on and you are likely to be asking questions informed by newer knowledge, different contexts and affected by contrasting experiences. The best way to find an appropriate answer to a new research question is to collect data designed to answer that specific question. Unfortunately, many secondary data sets inevitably do not encompass newer knowledge in their variables (in terms of question phraseology, parameterisation or conditionality), and so analysts must either (i) assume that the secondary data remain appropriate proxy measures, (ii) assume that newer knowledge is not important, or (iii) rephrase the research question to fit around existing data. However, moving our understanding forward often requires new data.

 Whenever you have a new, interesting research question that requires data that are slightly different from the norm, then one option is for you collect that data yourself. Relative to many data collection methods (such as time-consuming in-depth face-to-face interviews), questionnaires are a relatively cheap and quick way to collate a representative sample.

Whether your questionnaire is distributed by hand, in person or via the Internet, it is likely that the identity of the person is not of interest (after some self-disclosed socio-economic identifiers) and that you, the researcher, can ensure respondent anonymity. A benefit of guaranteeing respondent anonymity is that the respondents are more likely to answer the questions honestly and reliably, thereby enhancing the reliability and potential generalisability of your findings.

Academics should be pushing the boundaries of knowledge and not simply replicating the findings of others, even though that has its place. The most interesting research questions require us to collect new data and ask new unusual questions that are designed to uncover nuances in the literature. Even if your sample size is not sufficiently large to conform with some journals' expectations, it is entirely possible that you can change the course of research by discovering something that stimulates others to research a topic differently. Be curious and probe those research areas that remain underexplored; you might reveal something that is ground-breakingly different!

 Research leaders need to encourage their colleagues to think outside of the box and to pursue interesting and innovative ideas; this may require new evidence and new data. When reviewing each other's work, try to ask searching questions that establish the stability of existing results and explore nuances in the data. By doing this, research leaders might stimulate their colleagues to think in a new, previously unknown way, and hence they would be inspiring their colleagues and making a credible contribution to the life of your department.

Research leaders should make themselves available so that their colleagues can ask for guidance on the appropriateness of the wording of questions in questionnaires. Being a sounding board is a vital role of the research leader and can save colleagues time and effort later when they approach other academics who may be more informed on a specific research topic.

24. Interviews

Questionnaires and secondary data sometimes do not provide information in sufficient depth. It may be necessary for you to collect your own detailed data by conducting interviews (structured, semi-structured or open). Interviews can generate lots of extremely useful and deep information that can provide answers to your 'why' questions, which may not be answerable using other data collection methods. However, interviews can generate data that are heavily biased because the interviewee may inadvertently skew the respondents' answers. An excellent interview technique is required to extract the best data with the least bias.

Helper (2000) identifies four benefits of field research, including interviews.[1] First, the researcher can ask direct questions about their objectives and constraints, which are not always present when using secondary data that reflects outcomes. Second, fieldwork allows for the exploration of areas with little pre-existing data or theory, and therefore there is the possibility of garnering a much wider range of data. Third, fieldwork facilitates the use and sourcing of the right data, while secondary data might be inappropriate for the research question (or worse a researcher might still use secondary data and an incorrect answer). Fourth, fieldwork provides vivid images that promote intuition, and hence a reader can visualise the issue and more fully understand the perspective of the author. Helper emphasises that there are other issues that need to be ameliorated in order for fieldwork data to be acceptable, including the need to ensure that the data is as objective as possible (in a world where every social thing is partly subjective), as replicable as possible and as generalisable as possible (assuming that your research is designed to be generalisable and not a case study).

Interviews should be undertaken whenever you wish to improve understanding of and be in a position to better explain a phenomenon. When I have used interviews, I have always been astonished by the nuances and heterogeneities in the information provided by the interviewees, the differences between our core theories and practice, and the gap between what we teach and the nature of reality.

Interviews can be of two main types. Open-ended interviews can generate extremely rich data based around a conversation that goes in the direction that the interviewee wishes to go, and these are often used in ethnographic studies. Semi-structured interviews follow a path whereby the interviewer follows a rough script but can jump forward or backwards depending on the answers provided by the interviewee, so long as information on the majority/all topics is collected. Application of the semi-structured interview method tends to facilitate the collection of core data while allowing for additional meanderings in the conversation in order to collect extra information that has additional or unexpected relevance.

Contrary to many economists who insist on only applying econometric and mathematical models and rarely go into the field, the father of modern economics, Adam Smith (1776),[2] famously ventured into the field to visit a pin factory. Perhaps the apparent reduction in the frequency of application of this research method is because of the time-consuming nature of the method or because the correct application of the interview research method can be very difficult. The skills required to conduct a very high-quality interview are difficult to accrue without informed guidance, reflection and lots of experience. The best interviewers are able to put the interviewee in a comfortable position where they are able to reflect appropriately and accurately on their own experiences. In the main, this comfortable position is dependent on the rapport and degree of trust that exists between the interviewer and the interviewee.

 Many academics appear to only use one or two research methods, perhaps informed by their doctoral training and prior experiences. However, the best researchers are responsive to the content of the research question and the gap in the literature, and they are reflective enough to know which method(s) is (are) going to be the best for garnering the most appropriate data.

A research leader should know a range of research methods and be willing to assist and guide less experienced researchers towards the correct implementation of the most appropriate method for a research question. They should encourage their colleagues to venture into new methodological approaches, when relevant, and encourage them to capture more in-depth information as required by the research question. Interviews are often excellent ways to identify new issues or changes in the importance of already-established issues. Research leaders should highlight gaps in knowledge, often brought on by the repetitive application of the same methods, and suggest new methods to gather new insights, with interviews being one particularly good method. Research leaders should also lead by example, perhaps even showcasing their reflexive and agile approach to research and research methodology.

NOTES

1.   Helper, S. (2000), 'Economists and field research: "you can observe a lot just by watching"', *American Economic Review*, 90(2), pp. 228–32.
2.   Smith, A. (1776), *An Inquiry into the Nature and Causes of the Wealth of Nations*, W. Strahan and T. Cadell.

25. Focus groups

Choice and behaviour are guided by perceptions, opinions, beliefs and attitudes, but they are also appreciably affected, moulded and guided by our peers. Socially informed beliefs can be identified using a focus group where members are asked to openly discuss a topic with others. Although interviews can be effective and detailed, they tend not to be as conversational, explorative, controversial and opinionated when compared to a focus group setting. These types of conversational interactions can be useful to gauge the importance of peer effects in decision-making and when attempting to assess whether patterns of interaction differ depending on the proximity and size of a peer group. Focus groups can be used to reveal some really interesting naturally occurring feelings and biases that shape people's behaviour in the real world.

 This research method can be very useful when uncovering peer pressure-related information per se, and its application can be particularly revealing when trying to reveal how (in) appropriate it is to record information on an a priori scale. For instance, an isolated respondent's answers recorded using a Likert scale could differ substantially from when the same issue is discussed openly with peers.[1]

When a researcher implements a mixed-methods approach, such as focus groups, they can assess the importance of unknown biases in the data through method triangulation. If you wish to identify how people really feel about things, how they see the world in a slightly different way than others and how their perceptions and actions may be swayed by others, focus groups allow you to raise and then record these nuances.

 Try to apply this research method whenever you are particularly interested in attitudes and opinions that may differ between individuals and may be influenced by peer effects. Whenever you wish to understand mindsets and motivations, feelings and frustrations, or outlooks and opinions, try implementing a focus group in your research methodology.

My first experience of running a focus group required me to take the role of a dual moderator, whereby one of us asked questions and the other made sure that the questions were answered. This focus group activity ended up being so engaging and vibrant that we became duelling moderators in order to stimulate extra debate and reactions on contending perspectives. The application of this research method can be surprisingly enjoyable and fun; just make sure that you don't get too carried away!

 Research leaders need to make sure that their department achieves its potential, and this can require them to encourage their colleagues to increase their lateral thinking. Holding a focus group with appropriate respondents is one way to generate new research ideas. However, it is also the case that journals in some social science disciplines are less likely to publish articles that use focus groups, seemingly simply because that method is not one that the readership will be naturally familiar with. Nevertheless, focus groups can be run to firm up an idea or to find new ones, and therefore they should be a method that is used frequently by academics in many social science disciplines, and therefore should always be encouraged by a research leader.

One useful way to integrate colleagues is to establish a group of colleagues who can look at, for example, a questionnaire that will be used by another colleague in a particular piece of research. Installing an open and collegiate culture within a department whereby everyone is able to support and provide constructively critical feedback on another's impending research can strengthen a department, and these collegiate focus groups could be administered by the research leader.

NOTE

1. Brown (2010) finds significant contradictions between perceptions and reality in her study of well-educated managerial women when using a mixed-methods approach. She finds that the positive views received via surveys in response to statements like "My workplace supports working mothers" contrasts strongly with answers in interviews. Moreover, surveys are less able to capture nuances such as the inter-relationships between factors, the relative weighting of factors in decisions and their potential cumulative influence (Lightbody, 2009). See Brown, L. (2010), 'The relationship between motherhood and professional advancement: perceptions versus reality', *Employee Relations*, 32(5), pp. 470–94; Lightbody, M. G. (2009), 'Turnover decisions of women accountants: using personal histories to understand the relative influence of domestic obligations', *Accounting History*, 14(1–2), pp. 55–78.

26. Give students your ideas for projects

One thing that frequently surprises me is the inability of academics to interact with research students effectively. Naturally, I've written a number of papers with PhD students, but what may seem surprising to some academics is that I have also co-authored papers with Masters and even undergraduate students. Although the ability, interests and inquisitive nature of students varies substantially across and within educational levels, I have found that the more seriously I engage with my research students, the more ideas that I am able to give them. When both the student and the staff member are highly engaged with a common piece of research, we are more able to inspire each other, and I am then able to provide more guidance and encouragement to help them to progress and uncover something in their own research that is worth reporting.

 In many cases, engaged and interested students try harder and generate their own ideas. While many of those ideas simply reinvent the wheel, their contrasting experiences can add to the literature, so long as we recognise the nuances of their argument.

I have found it very worthwhile to provide those students with my own ideas and to talk openly about the research topic with each other as equals, as sometimes they contribute something different or follow a nuanced line of thought that can mould those ideas into something distinctive.

In other cases, I have given research students ideas about how to build on their own questions, and in some cases those students have gone out to collect primary data to rigorously test those ideas using state-of-the-art techniques.

This guidance has inspired them to find out something new, and when they are open to collaboration and to us polishing their research, then that research can turn out to be a co-authored journal article. Interacting with research students can be mutually beneficial.

 Tread this path selectively. Some students may initially appear very able but later experience inertia and a lack of agility. There are times when interacting with and recognising the potential in your research students can result in you putting in efforts to open doors of opportunities for them, such as a PhD student position. They could then work on something that is mutually interesting and you can encourage them to achieve their potential.

A research leader should be using their experience to recognise the research potential in undergraduate and postgraduate students. They should be opening doors for those students who are highly inquisitive, rough diamonds in order to maintain the vibrancy of the department. PhD students who are only undertaking PhD research in order to gain access to an academic job tend to conform more to the literature and add less vibrancy and inquisitiveness to the department. Those PhD students who are engaged in real-life research and wish to push the discipline forward should be supported and encouraged to learn the ropes while being innovatively disruptive to the literature. Disruptive innovation can have the greatest benefit and inspire that important step change that a theory, understanding or discipline needs, and sometimes these step changes are made by people who are new to the discipline and bring in desperately needed new ideas.

27. Anthropology

Applications of an anthropological research approach can be overlooked in the social sciences. Perhaps this is because data were not available at enough points in time across a population's historical evolution, or perhaps this is because the focus of discussion is squarely on the current point in time. Nevertheless, when we recognise that our behaviours are driven by our prior experiences and contexts, then it appears obvious that the research approach must have some credence. This approach can focus on cultural meanings, as well as institutional social norms and values. The tracing of people's lives can reveal some ways of thinking and knowing that strongly question conventional wisdom.

 One example of the anthropological approach is the work by Hughes (2021).[1] Hughes identifies whether Richard Florida's (2003)[2] findings that members of the creative class are attracted to a place because of the leisure amenities and community on offer. By interviewing key people who significantly shaped the evolution of the Bristol and Bath creative community, Hughes found that serendipity, childhood memories and coincidental events all resulted in the evolution of their prior migration, and not simply a human capital-based, wage maximisation process. Such deep and meaningful results could only have been identified through a process tracing, anthropological approach to data collection.

Greater usage of process tracing and anthropological research approaches could seriously question our ability to assume away serendipitous and seemingly irrelevant issues that are difficult to include in formal models. Drawing on anthropological studies could seriously improve your knowledge of the real world!

 There is no existing knowledge that clearly states when we should implement an anthropological-based research method. However, even when we are searching for meanings in our static, cross-sectional studies, it could well be the case that the variation across subjects reflects prior experiences, interpretations and variations between contexts, entry into which may themselves be a reflection of those prior experiences.

The important point may be to remain open to the possibility that a single research approach is inherently wrong and that a triangulation of research methods is superior. When we should use an anthropological approach is therefore difficult to ascertain, so be careful not to dismiss this approach too quickly. One answer to when we should use such an approach is offered by Pike et al. (2016),[3] who argue too that such a thorny matter needs to be embedded into research practices and supported by greater openness.

 Research leaders should not only be excellent at their own area of research but must also be agile enough to draw on their knowledge of other methods. Whether they use an anthropological argument to constructively criticise someone's research or use a different approach to question an anthropological approach is therefore innocuous; the important thing is that research leaders are acutely aware of the benefits of implementing different methods and can use those methods effectively to support and critique their colleagues' work and the established literature more generally.

NOTES

1. Hughes, E. (2021), 'Patterns of creative worker migration across the lifespan: the migration and occupation paths of Bristol designers, 1950–2018', PhD thesis, University of the West of England.
2. Florida, R. (2003), *The Rise of the Creative Class*, Basic Books.
3. Pike, A., MacKinnon, D., Cumbers, A., Dawley, S. and McMaster, R. (2016), 'Doing evolution in economic geography', *Economic Geography*, 92(2), pp. 123–44.

28. Open your eyes!

It is amazing that some academics do *not* recognise something relevant to their research in everyday casual encounters, be it something in the news, an encounter in a shopping centre or an event on holiday. Evidence of socio-economic change is all around us, including new norms and trends associated with advertising and marketing, new words entering languages, new health concerns and evolving socially influenced returns to education. All of these issues, and many more, shape our experiences, expectations and values.

As social scientists, the earlier we are able simply to recognise these issues, the earlier we are able to understand the true significance of the underlying mechanisms shaping our world and the earlier we are able to respond to them to reduce their adverse severity or to enhance any benefits.

Some of the most cited research is the easiest to relate to and understand. By drawing on examples that our readers relate to, we are able to make a point more easily and that point will transfer faster into consciousness. Embedding real-world examples into your theoretical paper can ensure that the reader recognises the relevance of your ideas faster and may enable them to assimilate your ideas into their work quicker, thereby enhancing your contribution to knowledge.

All the time!

The more I see, the less I know for sure. (John Lennon)

A research leader needs to make sure that their colleagues do not close themselves off in their ivory towers, and instead should ensure that their colleagues remain grounded in the real world. Some of the most trivial additions to academic literature seem to be based on ideas that could only have been dreamt up away from the real world.

Most of us have read papers that we cannot understand or comprehend why they were even published, simply because the contribution is unclear or incredibly trivial. Such papers include those that conclude that wage disparities exist, or that there are variations in levels of job satisfaction, or that houses with more bedrooms are sold for a higher price (see Aspinal, 2012).[1]

A research leader needs to provide guidance in order to strengthen the substantive contribution of their colleagues' research output, so that the full meaning of the research more easily permeates into the consciousness of policymakers and so that all academics pay something important back to society. Opening our eyes to the real world and seeing something interesting should stimulate us to try to answer the 'why' question.

NOTE

1. Aspinal, P. A. (2012), 'On avoiding research into the blindingly obvious', *Architectoni*, 1, pp. 74–82.

29. Relax assumptions

Many researchers approach their investigations by assuming the presence of an underlying mechanism or by assuming the absence of confounding issues. Although this may be convention in some disciplines, and therefore appear to be scientifically sound, in practice we rarely know enough about whether and how much our assumptions bias our models and/or interpretations, and hence our understanding of society.[1]

When social scientists investigate problems, conduct analyses and offer possible policy options, they look at the position of individuals and their array of outcome choices. However, the choice that someone makes is only the visible final step(s) of a comprehensive series of considerations (Scheuer, 2018),[2] which are often much deeper and frequently more challenging and interesting to understand than our oversimplified models. Assuming someone acts rationally does not enable the inclusion of the many paths of deliberation and reflection that an individual may take. Humanistic reflections on the perceived or real barriers created by an institution, social norms or in the mind of the individual are of prime importance when attempting to understand socio-economic behaviours.

Researchers from the Austrian School are particularly good at dissecting motivations and the roots of decision-making and social actions. Although their methods of analysis – typically praxeology or subjectivism – are arguably problematic for generalisation purposes, the depth of thought and understanding of the individual is arguably superior to many other approaches. Other researchers could benefit a lot simply by recognising the strengths of the Austrian approach and integrating elements of it into their own research.

Birks (2015) emphasises that assumptions are necessary for abstraction but that there is also a need to relax these assumptions if we wish to generate knowledge that is useful for real-world policymaking.[3] He recognises and underscores that the links between theory, empirical formulations and the real world are multifaceted, and that researchers should engage with these issues in much more depth.

Although model building obviously has its place within the social sciences, of much greater regard should be research that seeks to identify if/how this knowledge can be used for the benefit of society. Theoreticians have some amazing strengths, but they need to be integrated into a team that applies these theories to world issues. Understanding when (and why) a policy does work and how the benefits can be leveraged to benefit more in society should be a core aim of social science research. So, when should social science researchers consider relaxing assumptions? The answer should be all of the time.

 A research leader should ensure that their own work relaxes assumptions so that they increase its relevance to the real world, and they should encourage this reflection and model deconstruction in their colleagues' work. Research leaders must ask questions about and highlight the restrictive implications of underlying assumptions in their own and in their colleagues' work. They should question openly and constructively their colleagues' work in order to enhance its validity and practical usefulness, and they should encourage their colleagues to repay this compliment.

NOTES

1. Ask yourself: what kind of a social science starts with abstract assumptions from which it deduces its pre-ordained timeless truths, rather than being built on observable behaviour? How valid and useful can that knowledge and insight be for understanding our real world?
2. Scheuer, T. (2018), 'Computational agents, design and innovative behaviour: hetero economicus', *Economic Thought*, 7(2), pp. 82–94.
3. Birks, S. (2015), *Rethinking Economics: From Analogies to the Real World*, Springer.

30. Talk to Joe Public and try to understand their views

You may be surprised at how many of your non-academic friends and acquaintances find your research genuinely interesting. Few of us inflict them with the depth of our research thoughts, and this is a pity because when we try to express our research in non-technical language it can encourage us to simplify the issue, which in turn can generate simple and effective solutions to the obstacles and barriers that have been slowing the pace of our research. It is good to talk, but take note of their interest levels and stop before you bore them!

 Discussing my research with non-academic friends has solved my research problems on a number of occasions and encouraged me to think through my ideas in ways that I would not normally follow. Thinking about a research topic in slightly different ways can enable you to proceed with your own research more rapidly.

People say I have created things. I have never created anything. I get impressions from the Universe at large and work them out, but I am only a plate on a record or a receiving apparatus – what you will. Thoughts are really impressions that I get from outside. (Thomas Edison)

One set of connections that we should engage with frequently are policy-makers. One of my own core research interests focuses on local economic development, so the opportunity to discuss these ideas with local and national policymakers can improve my understanding of the spatial, social and temporal contexts that moderate and mediate the role of policies. It is possible to explore the location-specific relevance of these contextual issues, and hence drive research forward. Being open, informed and humble with policymakers can lead to more collaborative research opportunities, which enhances the potential positive impact on society.

 There are cultural, social, political and educational barriers that prevent interaction between academics and Joe Public. Allowing these barriers to inhibit effective knowledge sharing is unfortunate, especially when academics are too aloof to communicate effectively, when Joe Public incorrectly feels subordinate to academics or when Joe Public perceives academics as arrogant. These barriers, real or imagined, need to be broken down and effective communication streams need to be established if knowledge flows are to be maximised to benefit both the real world and academe.

Even when you are not conducting authorised interviews or undertaking ethically approved primary data collection, it is impossible to distance yourself totally from your own research interest and not recognise the daily relevance of some issues. Informally asking a shopkeeper whether they noticed a real drop in takings during a mega sporting event, and whether they perceive that their takings are simply reallocated away from particular event days, is useful small talk; you are simply showing interest in their business, and often people like to talk casually about themselves.

 Research leaders should showcase that they have a good understanding of real-world social science, and one way to do this is to relate their research to everyday life. By illustrating to their colleagues and to Joe Public that it is expected that social scientists do not simply sit in their ivory towers inventing theories that only work in a hypothetical world, research leaders can discourage some of their new career colleagues from trying to achieve (perhaps unconsciously) just that.

I once had a colleague that I thought should benefit from a better grounding and link to the real world, so I took that colleague for a coffee via the shop on the university grounds. During the walk I highlighted occurrences when their theory was reflected in real life and when interesting discussions with, for instance, the shop assistant ended up questioning the extent that their theory holds. This simple illustration highlighted to my colleague that their research was being experienced all around them and that further interesting questions (or different answers to existing questions) could be generated simply through greater conscious interaction with Joe Public. Highly research-active colleagues need to be grounded in reality, and the research leader has a responsibility to make sure this regrounding occurs at a frequency that is to the benefit of the researcher and hence to the research output of the entire department.

PART IV

Extra training expands minds

Training expands minds and this is required if you wish to make significant progress with your research. Training is useful in itself, as it increases morale, enhances a sense of achievement (Jones et al., 2009)[1] and job satisfaction (Georgellis and Lange, 2007),[2] enhances motivation levels, can make you think about your research topic in a new and potentially different light than your peers, and therefore increases your capacity to innovate.

Prioritise training rather than trying to push your research project slightly further forward in the short term. Attend training events even when they do not appear to have clear and immediate benefits to your current research. We know that it is easier to learn something from someone else than it is to invent new knowledge, so take advantage of the fact that "Everyone you will ever meet knows something you don't" (Bill Nye), learn from them, integrate that knowledge into your own research, and then push the boundaries of knowledge.

There is a range of areas where training can be beneficial to the research output of a department. Here are some training areas that appear to be particularly pertinent.

NOTES

1. Jones, M. K., Jones, R. J., Latreille, P. L. and Sloane, P. J. (2009), 'Training, job satisfaction and workplace performance in Britain: evidence from WERS 2004', *Labour*, 23, pp. 139–75.
2. Georgellis, Y. and Lange, T. (2007), 'Participation in continuous, on-the-job training and the impact on job satisfaction: longitudinal evidence from the German labour market', *International Journal of Human Resource Management*, 18, pp. 969–85.

31. Econometric and other quantitative methods training

Quantitative methods seem to be misunderstood by some academics who are expert in using these methods. Contrary to the understanding of some quantitative social scientists, the purpose of using statistical, econometric and other quantitative methods is not to showcase your numerical expertise, nor to conform to peers' methodological expectations, nor to generate an ability-related knowledge gap to exclude those who do not understand the method. Pushing this point to an extreme, Mark Blaug (1997, p. 36) argued that

> Modern economics is "sick." Economics has increasingly become an intellectual game played for its own sake and not for its practical consequences. Economists have gradually converted the subject into a sort of social mathematics in which analytical rigor as understood in math departments is everything and empirical relevance (as understood in physics departments) is nothing. If a topic cannot be tackled by formal modeling, it is simply consigned to the intellectual underworld ...[1]

Notwithstanding the critical importance of Blaug's perspective for the progress of economics and some other disciplines, the whole point of applying a research method is to push knowledge forward in a way that enhances our understanding of the real world. Quantitative methods are extremely useful for identifying averages or patterns in strings of data. For instance, these patterns can lead to the empirical identification of things that we did not know we did not know, or they can be used to establish the local context of a particular research issue. Understanding the context in which the research was undertaken is vital for the accurate understanding and communication of research conclusions.

Quantitative methods should be at least partially understood by all of the academic community, and this includes a comprehension of their limitations. Unfortunately, quantitative methods cannot *prove* a particular relationship exists in exactly the same way that a qualitative method cannot prove an effect either.[2] All research methods applied in the social sciences simply provide evidence that something is, or is not, consistent with one or more theories within the data frame.

There appears to be no end to the range of useful quantitative methods and additional statistical tests that we can apply in our research, and there are distinct tribes who prefer particular approaches (e.g. classical versus Bayesian regression). It is impossible for academics to keep up with all of the new developments in quantitative research approaches (with the possible exception of masterminds such as Professor Nicholas Cox[3] at Durham University, or Professor William Greene[4] at New York University Stern School of Business).

An effective way of ensuring that you stay abreast with at least some of the new developments in this field is to attend statistical and econometric training workshops taught at a pace comfortable for delegates. Two excellent examples that I have experienced include Professor Paul Voss's workshop on spatial regression using GeoDa[5] software and Professor Kelvin Jones's multilevel regression workshop using MLwiN[6] software. Such workshops provide opportunities to discuss issues with fellow delegates or with the lecturers in order to enable effective learning so that the methods can be applied appropriately when you return to your own office post-workshop.

 Several nudges can encourage you to update your knowledge of econometric and statistical methods. One nudge comes from others' feedback on your work. Another nudge comes from the realisation that a colleague is pushing their own quantitative abilities forward as they have self-trained or attended a training session, and that you too should follow suit. Constructive feedback on research presentations and useful referee reports from journal submissions both provide additional nudges and motivation to learn new and apply different, relevant techniques.

A further reason to keep up to date with your awareness of new quantitative techniques is to ensure that you can apply a method that your peers (and your referees) expect you to apply. As alluded to by Blaug above, part of this may be driven by social pressures within the discipline itself, but that doesn't necessarily stop you from also applying a method that you feel is more relevant to your research question.

If you have the knowledge to apply a particular method and agree with your peers, then you can either do the estimations yourself or ask an informed colleague to help you. A high level of knowledge about why the method is inappropriate to answer your research question is perfectly acceptable if you are able to constructively criticise the use of the method for your research, but you still need to have that knowledge in the first place.

 It is not unusual for research leaders to excel in the use of quantitative techniques, especially in seemingly more quantitative disciplines, like economics. After all, many journals appear more likely to publish papers that use quantitative techniques, especially when the result is articulated in a way that makes the reader think the result occurred beyond the possibility of random chance.

We all know that the more journal articles (especially in high-quality journals) an academic publishes, the more likely they will be promoted. However, the subsequent promotion of someone to a Head of Department or research leader position based on their own publication success is not going to guarantee the effective running of a department, partly because effective social skills that bring colleagues together and nurture their development are more important.[7] A cross-section of relevant skills is needed for promotion to senior positions, rather than simply being an expert in a method that is favoured within a discipline. If quantitative skills are not the strength of the research leader – which is perfectly acceptable – then they should know where their colleagues can obtain guidance on and develop their quantitative skills should they wish to do so.

NOTES

1.   Blaug, M. (1997), 'Ugly currents in modern economics', in Maki, U. (1997), *Fact and Fiction in Economics: Models, Realism and Social Construction* (pp. 35–56), Cambridge University Press.
2.   "The application of mathematics to economics has proved largely unsuccessful because it is based on a misleading analogy between economics and physics. Economics would do much better to model itself on another very successful area, namely medicine, and, like much of medicine, to adopt a qualitative causal methodology" (Donald Gillies).
3.   See https://www.dur.ac.uk/geography/staff/geogstaffhidden/?id=335.
4.   See http://people.stern.nyu.edu/wgreene/.
5.   See https://spatial.uchicago.edu/geoda.
6.   See http://www.bristol.ac.uk/cmm/software/mlwin/.
7.   Benson et al. (2019) emphasise that the best worker is not always the best candidate for a managerial position. See Benson, A., Li, D. and Shue, K. (2019), 'Promotions and the Peter principle', *Quarterly Journal of Economics*, 134(4), pp. 2085–134.

32. Qualitative methods training

Just like quantitative methods, qualitative methods cannot prove something exists. Whereas quantitative methods are typically there to identify averages or patterns across strings of data, qualitative methods are there to probe deeper in order to get closer to an understanding of an underlying mechanism.

Although some academics voice concerns over the generalisability and validity of qualitative data, the depth of information gained from qualitative methods tends to far exceed quantitative secondary data sets. One simplistic question to answer is therefore whether you prefer the generalisability of results or greater depth of understanding; of course we need both, so we need to gain a thorough understanding of qualitative methods too, and one without the other will always be problematic. Some academics emphasise that a mixed methods approach is superior and should be the approach that we aspire to adopt.[1]

 Training in qualitative methods can bring unquestionable benefits, and can reveal the true strengths and depths of qualitative data. Equally, some qualitative researchers perceive quantitative contributions to have only limited, if any, substantive relevance, especially when variations in contexts drive a spuriously accurate quantitative result.[2] Removing the blinkers worn by both sets of analysts can widen their scope of understanding of the limitations and strengths of all research methods.

A thorough understanding of the context (spatial/cultural/social/temporal etc.) in which data were collected is vital to enable an accurate understanding of quantitative results, and this can only be enhanced through training and the breaking down of misconceptions often accumulated during our prior training. Being trained to correctly apply qualitative methods not only potentially increases the depth of understanding in our research and enables extra clarification, it can also improve the contextualisation and the scope of generalisability, and thereby ensure that quantitative findings are not applied willy-nilly.

 Qualitative methods should be understood by all of the academic community, and this includes a comprehension of the limitations of these methods. All research methods applied in the social sciences simply provide evidence that is, or is not, consistent with one or more theories.

Qualitative methods are relatively good at answering 'how' and 'why' questions. They are particularly good when trying to explore the depth of understanding of an issue or when ascertaining the nuances that could prove vital for the application of particular policies. Training in qualitative methods can be vital when attempting to identify when a quantitative result should be usefully and appropriately applied.

 Because of the depth of information achieved when applying qualitative methods, it is often the case that the sample sizes in qualitative studies are much smaller than for quantitative studies. For instance, National Statistical Agencies often provide access to datasets that have millions if not trillions of observations, whereas one semi-structured interview that I conducted lasted for 3½ hours.

There will be times when you do not know the answer to a specific research question, and up-to-date theory has not yet been applied to the reparameterisation of questions within surveys, so you may have no choice but to collect your own data. This lack of clarity, coupled with an open mind, may require you to explore the qualifications of information, and this can only be done effectively with thorough knowledge of the application of qualitative methods.

 Research leaders who have a solid background in qualitative methods can be exceptionally useful for a whole range of disciplines and, in my experience, are very underrated. A research leader should make time to constructively criticise and unpick others' research method designs and question the extent of their validity. This will help colleagues improve the quality of their research and the quality of the data that they collect. A key question research leaders should be asking their colleagues prior to their collection of data is: what are the gaps in the literature that this new data seeks to fill and how could that data be criticised? If the individual collecting that data can answer those questions very credibly, then they are halfway to making an important contribution to the literature, and the research leader has made their important contribution in pushing their colleague forward.

NOTES

1. Downward, P. and Mearman, A. (2007), 'Retroduction as mixed-methods triangulation in economics research: reorienting economics into a social science', *Cambridge Journal of Economics*, 31(3), pp. 77–99.
2. It is often quicker to write quantitative papers when secondary data is available, and this can result in an unwarranted inflated opinion of quantitative researchers over-and-above the credibility of qualitative researchers simply because they are likely to be cited in a greater number of papers. O'Reilly (1973) states that high performers perceive themselves as having higher levels of job-required ability than do poor performers. See O'Reilly, A. P. (1973), 'Perception of abilities as a determinant of performance', *Journal of Applied Psychology*, 58(2), pp. 281–2.

33. Offer training to expand others' minds

For those of you who work in an open and collegiate department, an excellent way to bring colleagues together even more and to increase understanding of each other's research approach is to run a methods-focused seminar series. There will be some, perhaps even half of a department, that excel in one particular method or approach. You could have a session on variance partition coefficients, grounded theory or topological data analysis.

The purpose of these sessions is to showcase a method so that colleagues can understand what a method is for, when it could be used, what the benefits of using it are and how to use it. Colleagues could then consider employing it in their own research, and they will be aware of the method when they referee a paper that applied that technique.

The worst thing that can happen is that someone will strengthen their resolve and understand why they will not adopt a perspective or technique; that's fine, some colleagues are dogmatic. At best, everyone could learn the benefits of a new approach that would otherwise have been ignored or trivialised.

When I ran these sessions at a previous university, they did, without fail, stimulate more interest in each other's research, enhance discussion and brought the department closer together. These sessions can be run across a whole campus and by a specialist department, such as a statistics or sociology department, but often these sessions need to be highly generic in order to cater for the interests of a wide range of staff. Sometimes it is better to run comparable ones within a department to ensure content validity.

If you are an expert within your own department on a particular research approach, then your colleagues will benefit from you showcasing that approach. When others do the same, you will benefit from their expertise. Sharing these skills strengthens the department and increases the cross-fertilisation of ideas, creativity and collegiality.

There is often a need for greater understanding of a particular method and a willingness to stay up to date with particular approaches and/or develop new methods. With strong collaboration of an excellent former colleague, I was able to develop a new set of methods based on the ideas of concordance and discordance to test for the strength and type of convergence of a time series of data, and also a method to identify the final steady state distribution of that dynamically changing distribution.[1] Running staff research method sessions that train colleagues in particular methodological approaches are a great way to stimulate thoughts on how to adapt existing methods or even to create a new method, and such sessions are most effective in bringing people together to co-author spin-off papers.

When you present a method in a general way to colleagues, they recognise the strength of the method and appreciate how the application of the method could make a contribution to their own literature. If they think they can work with you, they may approach you to see whether you could apply that approach to their data. If you do collaborate, do make sure that you teach them how to apply the method themselves rather than simply do the research for them, as you will want to build their research capacity rather than simply increase the amount of work that you do.

 Research leaders should seriously consider the collegiate benefits of running staff seminars on methods. For those who work on theoretical development and grounded theory, advertising this stream of seminars as 'methods' may make them think that it is not for them. So, instead, research leaders could initiate a training seminar series with a discussion of a text, such as Ziliak and McCloskey's (2008) view on the 'Cult of Statistical Significance'.[2] The research leader should be taking the lead and even present several sessions in the series, but they should also actively encourage colleagues to contribute to a staff seminar series on methods even when they are not sure that they can make a novel contribution.

NOTES

1. See Webber, D. J. and White, P. (2009), 'An alternative test to check the validity of convergence results', *Applied Economics Letters*, 16(18), pp. 1805–8; Webber, D. J. and White, P. (2007), 'Convergence towards a steady state distribution', *Economics Letters*, 94(3), pp. 338–41; Webber, D. J., White, P. and Allen, D. O. (2005), 'Income convergence across US states: an analysis using measures of concordance and discordance', *Journal of Regional Science*, 45(3), pp. 565–89; Webber, D. J. and White, P. (2003), 'Regional factor price convergence across four major European countries', *Regional Studies*, 37(8), pp. 773–82.
2. Ziliak, S. T. and McCloskey, D. N. (2008), *The Cult of Statistical Significance*, University of Michigan Press.

34. Teacher training

Researchers can classify teaching as a second-tier duty and misunderstand the complexities involved in teaching effectively. Effective teaching techniques can be transferable to research, and particularly the presentation of research findings. Researchers that are most recognised for doing the best quality research are often those who are able to sell their research on stage, especially as researchers tend to reference people that they wish to be associated with. Therefore, acquiring techniques that enhance your teaching prowess will also enhance your ability to transfer your ideas on the research stage.

Contrary to popular belief, effective lecturers do not only need a strong grasp of the associated literature; they also need to have the right attitude, to adopt the right behaviours and to use the right basket of skills at the appropriate time for an audience.

Attitudes are acquired through experience, but they can be based on the 'wrong' experience; for example, you might have experienced a rowdy, unhelpful and unconstructive imposter at a conference, and this has made you cagey to reveal all of your recent theoretical developments and/or empirical findings – this helps no one. Behaviours are responses to various stimuli and can be involuntary and unconscious – awakening the consciousness of your behaviours can enhance your effectiveness in the classroom (and in life generally). Skills are multidimensional and include non-research related actions that influence others' impressions of the quality of your research.

Having a heightened awareness of your own attitudes, behaviours and skills enables you to increase your performance in the classroom and on stage at a conference. Most universities put on training sessions on a range of topics, and it is easy not to prioritise their attendance. But attending these teacher training sessions, and having this break from your research, can refresh your attitude to both research and teaching.

Two of the most memorable teacher training sessions that I attended were on the topics of teaching students who experience unseen barriers to learning, including being hard of hearing and being visually impaired. Both sessions changed the way I present at conferences and should make my talks more accessible.

Most researchers spend as much time as possible enjoying and participating in their own research, and they can forget that part of the impact of their research depends on how they 'sell' it. Taking opportunities to improve teaching prowess is therefore necessary. Unfortunately, in my experience, few researchers attend these sessions and instead they seem to be populated by colleagues on a teaching-only contract.

Teacher training sessions benefit researchers in the room, because the teaching skills in the peer group are most likely to be very strong, and these skills spill over to other colleagues within the training room. Researchers can then learn and adopt good teaching and communication techniques which have already been achieved by the teachers in the room.

Unfortunately, a lack of teacher training by some research-focused staff means that the communication of research in academic conferences can be very poor. For the sake of the impact of your own research, sign up for those teacher training opportunities and learn how to be a more effective lecturer, even if you treat the sessions as an opportunity to have downtime. There are also national accreditation schemes, such as the Higher Education Academy in the UK,[1] that can have other extrinsic benefits.

 Research leaders should encourage their colleagues to undertake teacher training. Effective teachers are able to inspire an audience and promote thought-provoking ideas that stimulate lateral thinking and insightful criticisms. These characteristics of effective teachers are also the desirable attributes of many effective and accessible researchers.

Many aspects of teacher training can be transferred from the classroom to the conference room for the benefit of not only the delegates but also the speaker. The more open and inspiring a researcher is during their conference presentation, the greater the likelihood that conference delegates will approach them with stimulating and insightful comments and questions.

NOTE

1. See https://www.advance-he.ac.uk/. Membership of the HEA is increasingly important for UK academics, and this may make it more difficult for overseas academics to teach in the UK in the future. More senior membership of the HEA (climbing from FHEA through to PFHEA) has many benefits and is seen very positively across the sector.

35. Conference attendance is also training

Conference attendance is a vital part of your career and you should prioritise attending conferences irrespective of how much you do, or do not, enjoy them. Not only does conference attendance form and strengthen your social networks, it is also an opportunity for you to hone your presentation skills to fellow academics. Leading a research seminar to a well-informed and interested audience is considerably different from teaching students or the next generation of researchers. Understanding what your research peers expect can act as a whip to stimulate yourself into deepening your understanding of your research topic and/or adopting particular attitudes, behaviours and skills.

Once you have attended an annual conference several times, you will know some fellow regular delegates well enough to phone them out of the blue and pick their brains. These fellow researchers are likely to be interested in your research topic more than many of the colleagues in your own department. You must practise stimulating their minds so that they respect your ability to generate new ideas and new ways of thinking. Gaining a higher level of understanding of the literature requires highly nuanced communication skills not only to push the boundaries but also to preserve delegates' enthusiasm for and comprehension of your research. This can require a different communication vocabulary than you are used to using in front of your students and also in front of your immediate colleagues.

If you feel that your research is not developing fast enough to enable you to present something 'good enough' at your next conference, then you may be tempted not to present. When you opt out of attending a conference you lose the opportunity to hone important skills.

Conference attendance should be seen not only as an opportunity to showcase your own research, but also to further your personal knowledge of other areas of research and to strengthen your social networks. Attending conference seminars in your immediate research area may have immediate benefits, because it will stimulate your mind and curiosity in ways that other conferences may not. Nevertheless, attending conference sessions on other topics could also be highly beneficial, because they encourage you to think in different ways that could have unexpected pay-offs or could lead you to an awareness of a technique or perspective that you could pass on to a colleague.

Universities invest money in your conference attendance, and their return is greatest if you actively share your new knowledge across your department. You would want other people in your department to share their knowledge with you if it could benefit you, so be proactive and collegiate and share the knowledge wealth. Part of this could simply be to collect copies of conference papers or to pass on an invite to present in your own department's staff seminar series because you recognise the benefits that could accrue to others within your department.

 Research leaders should encourage and finance conference attendance to those who are able to present their department in a positive light (effective conference presentations, engagement and networking) and who can bring immediate benefits to their department (knowledge transfer, improvements in research output through useful conference feedback, etc.).

Conference attendance is an investment in the specific academic, but it should also have positive spillovers for part or all of the rest of the department. Colleagues venturing off to conferences, not least research leaders, should be mindful of asking interesting speakers to present in their own staff seminar series at a later date, so that their colleagues can also benefit from hearing the thoughts of an excellent speaker.

36. Conduct PhD/Masters' examinations

As you progress up the scholarly ladder, you will encounter increasing opportunities to examine PhD theses. These can be very time-consuming and should not be undertaken on a whim. These opportunities provide you with the chance to train your brain to think a bit deeper on a topic that you may not have thought about in a particular way before.

Masters and doctoral research students can be supervised at arm's length with meetings being functional and with a low level of engaged interaction. These supervisory meetings can also be deep, meaningful and inspiring moments for the student and the supervisors. When a supervisory relationship is strong, it can stimulate a lot of questioning and can widen minds. The supervision of research students should be seen as a positive opportunity for academic staff to question issues and methods that they may otherwise have easily accepted.

 The act of examining a PhD is an opportunity for you to welcome someone into the academic family and truly engage with their research in a thorough and thoughtful way. It is an honourable opportunity to 'pay it forward' and give someone else the focused attention and engagement that someone else gave to you when you sat your PhD viva. Examining a PhD thesis can alert you to alternative theoretical, philosophical and empirical approaches to answering a particular research question.

All of the PhD viva voce that I have examined have been highly engaging, dynamic and an engrossing experience that celebrated the work of the candidate. They are an honour to be part of, and a good examiner is one who is very proud to be part of the transition of the candidate from PhD student to post-doctoral scholar.

If, after reading the thesis, you don't think that you would be proud to say that you examined that PhD candidate's work, then do not proceed to the viva; you are filling the role of a quality controller after all. To be selected by a colleague or acquaintance to conduct the PhD viva is also a great honour in itself, as it illustrates the standing that the fellow academic holds you in.

Each thesis will take you several days to read and reflect on, and you may then need to spend a day getting to the destination university city, a few hours to conduct the examination, a few hours to network with the student's supervisors and wider team, and a further day to return home. Nevertheless, the examination of external PhD theses is an expectation of senior academics and such opportunities should be turned down rarely. They are an important opportunity for you to give back to the profession and to bring on the next generation of informed academics.

 Research leaders and full professors should be conducting internal and external PhD examinations on a regular basis, perhaps even two or three each year, depending of course on the number of internal PhD students and their external connections. But up and coming staff members should also be contributing by undertaking internal PhD examinations, perhaps once every other year when they are near to being promoted to or already are an associate professor. Research leaders should be on the lookout for opportunities for their less experienced colleagues and suggest roles and responsibilities if they think a particular colleague has the relevant skills and experience.

37. Undertake adventurous research

Research should be an adventure – train yourself to think this way. Celebrate the fact that you have the freedom to participate in research activities and be excited by the process. You are so lucky to be paid for doing something that you might have chosen to do as a hobby. This rollercoaster of a research adventure generates many ideas and, even though most of those ideas will inevitably fail, the experience of recognising that you may have nudged understanding that little bit further forward is very rewarding.

If you lose your motivation and if the experience permanently stops being a sense of adventure, then consider making a change in research topic, alter your own expectations of yourself or even switch your role, responsibilities and/or workplace.

Researchers can and should be adventurous in their research. It is okay to be adventurous in your lateral thinking! And it is much better to be regarded as a lateral thinker than as a person who simply applies others' ideas to specific cases. Of course, the latter has its important place within academe, as ascertaining the relevance of others' ideas to specific contexts can reveal new and important knowledge about the spatial, temporal and contextual transferability of ideas.

It takes reflection, feedback and constant learning, backed up by solid motivation, to generate real, innovative and interesting research output. The motivation to innovate is partly driven by our inner desire to contribute something new and meaningful, for whatever reason(s), but also by an inner drive and belief that something new is possible, and that is associated with a journey into the unknown and by the taste for adventure.

Try to think how someone else would approach your research topic. Attempt to answer your research question in a different way than you usually would, perhaps simply by following that inspiring idea that a speaker gave you in a recent staff seminar. Try to develop an unusual solution, and question why it is unusual and whether that matters. Sometimes it can be worthwhile trying to reverse-engineer things, as that can lead you to new thoughts and ideas. Work on something that is unpredictable and complex. Impose your own structure, if necessary, to make progress. Make sure that you face your own research fears head on and without hesitation. Being bold can allow you to progress faster with your research than if you progress along your usual path.

We can't solve our problems with the same thinking that we used when we created them. (Albert Einstein)

Go into the lion's den of research: present your research on purpose to people you know will not like it: this will stimulate you and train you to think about things from other people's perspective(s). (You will not be pushed enough if you simply present your research in front of sympathetic like-minds.)

Do something different in your personal life too. Our research lives are heavily entwined with our research journeys, and we very frequently reflect on our research during our personal downtimes. Do something that is inspirational in your personal life and it may stimulate you to think even more laterally in your research life. Being adventurous in your personal life can spark your research-related thoughts to work in a different direction. It will build confidence when you think outside the box.

When your mind is working overtime and generating some wonderfully original and creative thoughts, and this can be at work, a coffee shop, on a jog around the park or in the middle of a game of squash, make sure that you are prepared with either a notepad or your phone so that you can record them before you lose the idea. At a later date, you will often realise that those wild thoughts are bunkum, but every now and then they can be developed into something significant that you would have lost if you had not recorded it when you had the chance. Be adventurous in all your research areas; just think what you could learn from doing so and how many people could benefit from that knowledge. Society is relying on you to do this!

Research leaders should actively encourage and train colleagues to push their own research boundaries. Part of this encouragement and training can be achieved by teaching colleagues new ways of researching or encouraging open and lateral thinking through discussion using the 'what if ...' approach. At other times, a research leader needs to show their colleagues how they embrace a sense of adventure into their own research, perhaps by integrating into a staff seminar presentation how they used a 'what if' approach successfully in that piece of research.

The more we undertake research, especially from a pluralistic and deep approach, the more we realise that we do not know something with certainty. A research leader can employ the 'what if' approach in one-to-one coffee break or water-cooler chats simply by stimulating engagement through interesting anecdotal discussion. Research leaders should develop and train their social skills and knowledge to know how to feed their colleagues' aspiring minds with different morsels of information, or through the revelation of a contending perspective that will encourage them to question (perhaps in an adventurous way) what they have already done/are doing.

38. Attend talks and presentations on very different topics

Make time to attend something that appears potentially stimulating, albeit unconnected to your own research. University email distribution lists often contain notifications of forthcoming open seminars, training opportunities or other similar events. Try attending a session on the computational department's approach to artificial intelligence, the biology department's approach to unravelling DNA or the built environment department's approach to developing new towns. All of these can stimulate you to think differently about your own research topic, however detached, and often in surprising ways. This behaviour can also build your within-university network, and can pay off in unexpectedly beneficial ways, such as a future grant application written by them but where they need someone in their team with your specific skills.

 You never know when you need to draw on that extra knowledge or social network. Getting your name known across departments (and even across universities in your city region) can have major pay-offs. I was asked to fill an economist's role on an external grant application seemingly only because of my networking with members outside my department. That substantial and successful external grant funded an excellent PhD student, made new links to further academics and bought out teaching time that I could devote to further my own research.

 These training opportunities should not be your priority, but when you can afford an hour eating your lunch watching something different in the next department's staff seminar series, there may be a pay-off. It might push you to question your own research approach; it may make you think about applying their method to your own data; at worst, it gives you an hour to let your mind relax as you look out of the window so that you are revitalised and ready to return to research after the session.

 Some universities have a message board that informs everyone about the training activities on campus. When this does not happen, the faculty's research team (associated Dean or equivalent) should bring these diverse sessions to the awareness of colleagues. In the absence of this responsibility, the department's research leaders should take up the role.

Universities should be a place to share knowledge and make it available to all. Research leaders need to lead by example and make sure their colleagues are aware of opportunities in other departments. Research leaders should also attend these extra-departmental sessions as a matter of course, as they strengthen their intra-university networks and heighten awareness of their department across other departments.

39. Inter- and multidisciplinary engagements

Research questions are approached from different angles by researchers in different departments. For instance, the ontological and epistemological research approaches of sociologists and economists tend to be so different that such academics rarely communicate effectively with each other. Instead of being aloof and dismissing outright an alternative research approach adopted by someone in that 'other' department, try to engage with and understand why they approach the topic in a particular way. By properly appreciating others' approaches, either you will be able to justify more effectively why you are adopting your own approach, or you will move closer to that alternative method that may enhance your own research.

 Questioning your own philosophical and ideological research approach will make you a better researcher. Making connections between different concepts and approaches increases the grounding of the research in the real world, thereby enhancing the applicability and relevance of research.

Your research will become increasingly meaningful and funders will increasingly recognise it for being useful to them. It will enhance the depth of your research and simultaneously move you away from your ivory tower, thereby enhancing your value to the outside world.

People will become increasingly interested in your research, too. You will have more to say to more people, a wider range of people will want to talk to you and your value to the department, university and wider world will increase. Your critical thinking skills will improve and you may begin to think of more and a wider range of alternative ways of solving your own research problems. You may even start to ask research questions that have greater and more immediate relevance to the real world, and therefore increase the possibility of you making a positive impact on society.[1]

 Whether and when you should adopt an interdisciplinary approach to research will always be a moot point, and different people will respond to these questions at different points in their career. All points on this continuum have merit, but the points with most merit will depend on the context and timing of the question, background training of the academic, knowledge of the audience and the appropriateness of the underlying assumptions.

It is best to reduce those assumptions as much as possible, approach the research question from a variety of interdisciplinary social science perspectives and learn from the benefits that each approach provides. Even if you don't use interdisciplinary approaches in your own research, having an in-depth awareness of other social science approaches will strengthen your research.

Research leaders should be very open to interdisciplinary research, not only in their own research endeavours but also when helping to guide their colleagues' research efforts. However, having an inter- or multidisciplinary approach is beyond many very able and very senior researchers. A research leader does not necessarily need to know the answer to all inter- and multidisciplinary questions, but they do need to know someone who can help and be willing to be a constructively critical and supportive sounding board for those academics currently researching inter- and multidisciplinary topics within their own department.

NOTE

1. See Jones, C. (2009), 'Interdisciplinary approach: advantages, disadvantages, and the future benefits of interdisciplinary studies', *ESSAI*, 7(26), pp. 76–81.

40. Learn to eliminate distractions

Eliminating distractions requires you to turn off your mobile phone, stop reading emails, disengage yourself from social media and other news, and shut yourself away so that you do not engage in conversations. The single goal during an intensive research stint is to get as much done as possible in a short time. Training and allowing your mind to work in short stints, and going with the flow in an uninterrupted and intense block of time, can be of immense benefit to your research and be more fruitful than long stints of focused but draining effort, especially as the latter can lead to burnout.

 Working on two things at the same time will reduce your focus. It will enable your brain to interrupt one task with another, thereby making you less productive. Every time you switch between tasks, your attention and focus do not immediately return to its optimal level because part of your mind will continue to toil with the previous task. We are often spreading our efforts too thin.

> Take up one idea. Make that one idea your life – think of it and live on that idea. Let the brain, muscles, nerves, every part of your body, be full of that idea, and just leave every other idea alone. This is the way to success. (Swami Vivekananda)

Professor Menon at Stanford University[1] emphasises that multi-tasking is associated with switching costs from one task to another, which requires further time to reconstruct the problem in the mind. Professor Menon also suggests that there may be a trade-off between multi-tasking and creativity, so too much multi-tasking can reduce your creativity and reducing your multi-tasking may increase your ability to be creative in your academic writing.

 This problem has two sides: how do you stop distracting others, and how do you stop other people and things distracting you? The first requires you to be conscious that you are distracting them, and, at times, this is difficult, especially when you think that you are helping the person that you are distracting. The best thing to do in this situation is to accept their calm and polite suggestion that now is not a good time and that you should approach them with your suggestions later.

A good way to limit the ability of others to distract you is to anticipate disturbances and distractions and put a message on your door such as 'Please do not disturb. I will be available from X pm'. Surprisingly few people do this, but doing so facilitates a prolonged period of focus and informs the other individual when you will be available to talk to them at a later time.

Synchronise other effective blockers too by, for instance, turning your phone off, turning off your email and turning all other forms of communication off at key times of the day when you know that you are most proficient. I often do this for entire mornings, especially when colleagues seem to call by mid to late afternoon for casual chats, etc. It is best to be prepared.

 Research leaders should, again, lead by example, making it crystal clear that they are available frequently but that there will be times when they will not be available. Junior colleagues should learn from this 'visible non-availability' and safeguard their own time to ensure that they too progress with their research. Research leaders should encourage their colleagues to ring fence their time so that they can make significant advances in their thinking and highlight that this is best practice, as long as they also allocate time so that they are accessible and amenable to others.

NOTE

1.   See   https://news.stanford.edu/thedish/2014/09/30/stanford-psychiatrist-tells-us -why-it-is-good-to-daydream/.

PART V

Colleagues and collaborations

Throughout this book, I have attempted to emphasise that a supportive department with colleagues who are constructively critical and highly intrinsically motivated will be a more productive research-active department than one where incivility and gaslighting are rife between extrinsically motivated colleagues.[1] Who would you prefer to promote? And who would you prefer to work with?

There are ways to ensure that you benefit collectively from actions and behaviours. Schumacher (1973, p. 39) emphasised that we should have three work functions:

1. to give someone a chance to utilize and develop their faculties,
2. to enable them to overcome their egocentredness by engaging with other people in common tasks, and
3. to bring forward the goods and services needed for a better existence.[2]

The achievement of each of these functions seems to rest on the dignified and respectful integration of responsible colleagues in a way that encourages human ingenuity and effort. In line with that perspective, this selection of ten tips outlines areas which may increase the incidence of active and fruitful interactions within a department.

NOTES

1. Unfortunately, incivility, fear, ego and power, amongst other factors, all under-mine the establishment and deepening of such a positive and enabling research culture. To motivate change, therefore, we need to avoid generating fear which induces inaction, and instead enthuse the thrill of a gain because it induces action (Sharot, 2014). See Sharot, T. (2014), 'How to motivate yourself to change your behaviour', TEDxCambridge Talk, available at https://www.youtube.com/watch?v=xp0O2vi8DX4.
2. Schumacher, E. F. (1973), *Small Is Beautiful: A Study of Economics as if People Mattered*, HarperCollins.

41. Different people bring different things to a research team

Departments where the majority of members follow very similar ontologies, epistemologies and world views appear to generate less lateral thinking, experience less constructive criticism and can experience methodological monism (see, for example, Dusek, 2008).[1] Although working with others who think in a similar way can generate deeper ideas, it may be the case that the best way to understand and solve a problem is to approach it from different angles. When building a research team, it can be better to work with people with whom you can debate a topic with openness and understanding, rather than with fear of being wrong or experiencing imposter syndrome.

 Although Zenger and Lawrence (1989) argue that coordination costs in diverse teams reduce collective performance,[2] Lazear (1999) argues that if a team comes from a diverse range of cultures then it will benefit from greater collective knowledge and skills.[3] Bandiera et al. (2010) show that individuals who work with more productive peers become more productive themselves, and vice versa.[4]

 When we deliberate over a research problem or discuss a topic with colleagues, what we are attempting to do is make a link between items that are currently distant in our minds. Our thinking brings those ideas together to solve that problem or improve understanding. People with different backgrounds and research interests will contribute different ideas to a team, form different connections and should be recognised for their contributions. Contributions can be from quantitative analysts who like to be at the forefront of new methods, a qualitative interviewer who enjoys digging deeper, to a calm figurehead who can communicate effectively with the media and heighten the profile of their research team. All colleagues have a relative advantage in a particular skill, and potentially have an absolute advantage in a particular area too, and they should be encouraged to use them for the betterment of the department.

 Teams of colleagues appear to be most constructive and productive when members mutually respect each other and bring something extra to the conversation. Research leaders and other senior members of the department need to nurture an atmosphere that encourages colleagues to contribute to the achievement of the department's clear aims of producing high-quality research output.

This will involve active and mutually respectful communication that encourages and supports each other's contributions in a way that motivates each other to achieve their potential; a department comprising excessively competitive individuals who undermine each other's research activities appears to divide and demotivate the department and discourage the creation of positive research contributions. Colleagues who unconstructively, disapprovingly and destructively criticise rather than embrace and push forward each other's contributions need to be pulled up on that behaviour and if possible the research leader should try to discover where the behaviour originates and let the colleague know that it is not acceptable.

NOTES

1.   Dusek, T. (2008), 'Methodological monism in economics', *Journal of Philosophical Economics*, 1(2), pp. 26–50.
2.   Zenger, T. R. and Lawrence, B. S. (1989), 'Organisational demography: the differential effects of age and tenure distributions on technical communication', *Academy of Management Journal*, 32(2), pp. 353–76.
3.   Lazear, E. P. (1999), 'Globalisation and the market for team-mates', *Economic Journal*, 109(454), pp. 15–40.
4.   Bandiera, O., Barankay, I. and Rasul, I. (2010), 'Social incentives in the workplace', *Review of Economic Studies*, 77, pp. 417–58.

42. Work with people who you can learn from

Although research-focused departments appear to prosper when colleagues support and collaborate, it remains vital that all researchers continue to develop their own strengths and portfolio of skills to enhance the likelihood that they can make new discoveries. A researcher's first priority should be to make sure that they contribute to the pool of knowledge in the most effective manner, and an efficient way to do this is to learn new ideas, methods and ways of thinking from the colleagues around them.

 Today, one of your colleagues may need help solving a problem; tomorrow, it maybe you that requires that assistance. Some colleagues have not experienced the benefits of working collaboratively, and perhaps that is because their previous colleagues have not wanted to work with them or their previous work environment was not set up to encourage this type of working relationship. If you feel that you do not need any assistance and constructive discussion with colleagues from time to time, then either you are not pushing yourself hard enough or you fail to recognise the benefits of doing so. Working in isolation is likely to slow your progress and reduce the contributions that you can make to improve your understanding of the research topic; working collaboratively with people who you can learn from speeds up your lateral thinking skills and increases the sophistication of contributions that you make to society.[1]

 I have had the pleasure of working with some truly excellent researchers who do not share their research openly because they have worked in departments where their colleagues have trivialised those contributions (often because they do not understand their significance). Some researchers may be true innovators to our literature, especially when they care passionately about their contributions, but we may stunt their progress if we do not treasure them. Not taking the opportunity to learn from your colleagues not only reduces your own knowledge accumulation, but also stunts others' ability to contribute to your great idea and help it to fruition and publication, thereby reducing our ability to improve society and understand the social sciences more generally.

Many of us know both senior and junior researchers who are so in need of being recognised for their own parochial contributions that they feel compelled to diminish and belittle the contributions of others. They refuse to accept the importance of others' perspectives and appear to feel dogmatically that they must be right.

Research leaders should provide support to their colleagues so that they achieve their potential and surmount barriers, effectively reaching a state of self-actualisation.[2] Research leaders should be familiar with the benefits of listening to, appreciating and understanding their colleagues, not only to enlighten themselves but also to display a mutual respect that encourages interaction across the department, to support the generation of ideas and to do this frequently at impromptu moments.

Research leaders can encourage colleagues to learn from each other by encouraging them to share ideas of best practice and recognise that other researchers are, at a point in time, progressing with their research faster than they are. It is important for research leaders to understand that different colleagues respond to different stimuli and that different approaches are appropriate when supporting different colleagues' learning opportunities.

NOTES

1. Just as nomads of Mongolia invest in their knowledge of tradition, heritage and history, and pass that knowledge from generation to generation to create a rich tapestry and respectable set of communities, academics should do the same. See Batkhuyag, K. (2020), 'The ancient, earth-friendly wisdom of Mongolian nomads', TED Video, available at https://www.ted.com/talks/khulan_batkhuyag _the_ancient_earth_friendly_wisdom_of_mongolian_nomads?language=en.
2. Maslow (1970) finds that only a mere 2 per cent of people achieve self-actualisation, and yet arguably it is embedded and perhaps the only way to progress within in our profession. See Maslow, A. H. (1970), *Motivation and Personality*, Harper and Row.

43. Work with people who you can teach

Although you should ensure that you work in a culture where colleagues can learn from each other, it is vitally important that you are able to teach your colleagues something too. If you do not have anything to offer them, they will look for intellectual interaction elsewhere and you will not be able to strengthen the team.

Whether colleagues spend time listening to you will depend, at least in part, on whether they perceive that you have something to contribute to the team. You will strengthen a team when other people in your team perceive that you have something to offer them. This perception can be fortified or undermined by other colleagues within your department.

A team is likely to weaken in the long run if it is comprised of members who perceive that they can only learn from people external to the team. People may start to leave because they perceive more benefits outside of the department than from within. The more that you are able to offer your expertise to your colleagues and the more that you can teach them, the more expertise that they are likely to offer you. Knowledge sharing, listening carefully to each other, teaching each other different concepts and methods, training up each other's skills, offering support and ideas, and general togetherness will all energise the department and bring it together for mutual benefit. If you are unable to offer anything to your colleagues, the less they are likely to offer something to you.

If members of your team are not seeking your opinions to learn from you, it is time to self-reflect on why that might be; perhaps you are coming across as aloof, or your style may be confrontational or too passive. Perhaps ask a trusted friend or colleague for insight. Once you have identified possible issues, it is beneficial to consider changing the way you communicate with your colleagues in sending and receiving capacities. Alternatively, it may be the case that the group are not communicating effectively and that there are established underlying prejudices and a belief about others' potential contributions.

Effective teaching and communication enable others to identify your strengths, but this also requires active listening if the communication of ideas is going to be effective. Physically or metaphorically furled ears, sometimes linked with functional fixity but also linked with peer pressures, prevents the ability to learn from each other and discourages the willingness to teach each other too. Identifying how to impart your knowledge and how to increase the acceptance of that knowledge is vital for your personal growth and that of a department.

Try approaching issues from new angles (theoretically, ontologically, philosophically or empirically) and you may be surprised at what lessons you have to offer your colleagues. Encourage colleagues and collaborators to think differently or consider a different element of the problem. Being open to these new possibilities can be half the battle.

 Of course, colleagues can be welcoming or frosty, sometimes but not always on purpose. Senior colleagues, including research leaders, need to establish a culture that is open, calm, non-confrontational and engaging, so that learning from each other is encouraged.

Research leaders need to illustrate as clearly as possible that all colleagues are worth listening to, learning from and educating. This mutual respect will generate confidence and colleagues will realise that they can contribute to and learn from each other.

At the same time, an engaged research leader should identify the limits of colleagues' knowledge and try to fill those gaps. Positive encouragement will help colleagues grow intellectually, which will have long-term benefits for the team.

44. Work with people who you enjoy working with

Never forget that you are an incredibly lucky individual because you are doing a job that you (most probably) enjoy (part of it, at least). At any institution, it is imperative that people enjoy their research and their work more generally. My experiences confirm other anecdotal evidence that if you enjoy working at your institution, you are going to be engaged in your research to a higher level, perhaps due to fewer distractions. When you look forward to going to work, you will want to return to your research repeatedly. As we are social animals, colleagues can heighten the enjoyment of going to work and it is often a more enjoyable journey when you are sharing it with others. If you do not enjoy the company of colleagues in your department, look for collaborative opportunities in other department in your own institution or in other universities.

Research that builds on the work of Csikszentmihalyi (1997) has shown that work-related flow enhances self-efficacy beliefs, achievement and productivity.[1] Salanova et al. (2006) emphasise that work-related flow has a positive influence on personal and organisational resources, and hence greater enjoyment at work, and stronger work motivation enhances levels of personal and organisational success.[2] Others, such as Wright (2003), emphasise that positive organisational behaviour must include the happiness and health of employees as viable targets.[3] We spend almost a third of our adult life at work, so we may as well try to make choices that enable us to enjoy it.

If you are not enjoying the company of your colleagues or your place of work, then try to identify why that is the case and make a change. In some cases, it may simply be that you have outlived and outgrown your stay, and in other instances it will be because a colleague has a problem and they are taking it out on you. There are, of course, other reasons. Whatever the cause, do make a conscious decision to change for the benefit of your research. Avoid working with people who you find demoralising – you probably will not be alone in feeling this.

There are also initiatives that you can do to enhance the enjoyment of work for your colleagues. Sure, you will never be able to please everyone, but some of the time you will be able to increase enjoyment in the work environment.

I often run a small annual competition called 'Predict the Premiership' where people opt in to forecast the final positions of football teams at the end of the English Premiership season.[4] A monthly table emailed around to entrants generates a little fun camaraderie that stimulates uplifting conversation at the water-cooler. Other small contributions to the life of the workplace can work wonders for colleagues' morale.[5]

 Research leaders should undertake initiatives to bring colleagues together, to increase opportunities for them to get on with each other inside and outside of the workplace. This does not have to be in the form of a competition, as it could be a monthly communal lunch, weekly get-togethers in a bar after work or Monday morning coffee breaks. The most important aspects are that all colleagues feel that they can attend or join in, that it is an enjoyable experience and that colleagues do not feel that they must stand in rank and file.

Use these social occasions to break down barriers, reduce confrontations, calm the atmosphere and learn how to appreciate each other more. As academia is such a small place, where everyone seems to know each other, so the grapevine lets others know which institutions to avoid.

NOTES

1. Csikszentmihalyi, M. (1997), *Finding Flow: The Psychology of Engagement with Everyday Life*, HarperCollins.
2. Salanova, M., Bakker, A. B. and Llorens, S. (2006), 'Flow at work: evidence for an upward spiral of personal and organisational resources', *Journal of Happiness Studies*, 7, pp. 1–22.
3. Wright, T. A. (2003), 'Positive organizational behavior: an idea whose time has truly come', *Journal of Organizational Behavior*, 24, pp. 437–42.
4. Send Don an email if you wish to have a copy of his entry form and the rules of the game.
5. There is an abundance of literature that associates a worker's morale with their commitment to the firm (e.g. Bewley, 1999), typically based on the belief that a worker's satisfaction is founded on non-pecuniary variables in addition to monetary ones and effort (e.g. Akerlof and Kranton, 2005). See Bewley, T. F. (1999), *Why Wages Don't Fall in a Recession*, Harvard University Press; Akerlof, G. A. and Kranton, R. E. (2005), 'Identity and the economics of organisations', *Journal of Economic Perspectives*, 19(1), pp. 9–32.

45. Ask people to read your work

I am always surprised by how many colleagues do not do this! Everyone should get feedback on their papers before they send them to journals so that they do not waste the journal's referees' and their own time. A colleague will spot grammatical errors or clumsy phraseology much faster than you will yourself. Removing errors and enhancing the flow of the text will significantly enhance the enjoyment of the reader of the work, and so it is likely to increase the chance of publication too.

 There are several layers to this issue. First, once a paper is in full draft and good enough to submit to a journal, then is the time to start asking colleagues to provide feedback on your script. Error-strewn documents should not be distributed, as your colleagues will become frustrated and will not want to allocate their precious time to help you in the future. Typically, this first group of colleagues should be from within your own department and their role should be to ensure that your paper makes sense, is clear and that there are no obvious flaws in your argument.

Second, you should then ask your network of contacts who research a closely connected area to provide a pseudo-referee report on the document for you. The purpose of these revisions is to identify if there are reasons why an editor would desk reject the paper or whether there are obvious reasons for a referee to recommend rejection. The more people who you find to informally read and comment on your paper on a sequential basis so that efforts are not duplicated, then the greater the likelihood that the journal will request only minor changes and hence further enhance the likelihood of acceptance at the journal. It is useful for you to ask them to inform you whether you sell the paper enough to the referee and whether the substantive contribution of the paper is coming through strongly enough. Try to make sure those informal referees provide you with accurate guidance on which journal they would expect to see the paper in too, as this could ensure that you target the paper at the right outlet (not too high and not too low).

 The best way to create this network of informal peer review is to ask internal colleagues to review your papers and for you to repay the compliment. The most important thing to remember is that you are not infallible, that you are human and that you will make mistakes: this is inevitable if you are pushing the boundaries of social science. If you are not making errors, then you are not pushing the boundaries hard enough!

To minimise those mistakes, you should be able to rely on your colleagues to support and help you, and the best colleagues provide active guidance and constructively critical feedback to enhance the power of your argument. Try to use this collegiate network as much as you can.

Research leaders can initiate this type of collegiate support mechanism with new members of staff. They could install a behaviour in existing and new staff, a responsibility to assist each other by reading each other's manuscripts. A good way to do this is for research leaders to ask junior staff to provide comments on their work, who may be flattered that they were asked. If they agree, then they may be nervous about providing too critical feedback, and in this case it can be best to ask a straight question, like "Could you second-guess why this paper might be rejected please?" They will want to be seen to be performing, and they could bring a fresh perspective to your work. Once this internal review system is established and recognised as being mutually supportive, it will become second nature and will further bring a constructively critical department closer together and improve further the quality of research output.

46. Read and debate each other's work

Another way to bring colleagues together is to start a reading network and ask all members of the department to participate in the initiative whenever they can. A reading group can have two functions: first, it can be a place for the discussion of historically important, partially neglected, or newly published texts. Second, it can be a place where you discuss each other's texts in an attempt to assist each other's research progress.

 Being part of an informal refereeing group provides you with a range of benefits. First, it keeps you ahead of the literature so that you know what is being worked on before it comes out in journals. Second, it gives you an opportunity to hone your analytical skills and debate. Third, it can enhance your standing within that reading group, and the deeper, more insightful and helpful your comments become, so the more they will appreciate your skills. Fourth, your feedback may strengthen others' imagination and analytical skills, which could help move their research forward. Fifth, you could learn new analytical skills that you could integrate into your own work or it could stimulate collaboration with specialisation so that, say, they apply the research method and you contextualise and integrate the results into the literature. The only downsides of reading and commenting on someone else's work before it is sent to a journal are:

(i)   The paper may not be ready for your review (such as the grammar being too poor for you to understand), in which case tell them to polish the paper first and then you will review it properly.
(ii)   It will take you time to do it properly. It is better to give your colleagues an understanding of the timescale in which they will receive your feedback, rather than letting the paper sit in your inbox for months.
(iii) It may reveal to your colleague your lack of knowledge of the area.
(iv)   Sometimes you have to be honest that you did not like a piece of research, and that's perfectly fine if you communicate those ideas in a way that leads the author to improve the paper.

All of these downsides are acceptable if you are working with the right colleagues and if they are providing reciprocal support.

Proper informal reviews of all work should be carried out prior to any submission to journals. Unless you are already a world-leading contributor to the literature, then you are very likely to benefit from informal feedback. In fact, if you look at the first footnote of published papers of Nobel Prize winners, they often list many people who provided feedback on the development of the paper; perhaps the way to achieve such status and publish substantively important work is to gain feedback on it first!

 Research leaders must offer their time, informal refereeing skills and perhaps even training in providing this constructive feedback to all their colleagues. Experienced guidance will accelerate the pace of improvement of less experienced colleagues. Research leaders should help to establish reading networks and be aware of relevant networks for colleagues who have not yet found one.

Establishing a culture where we constructively, critically and thoroughly debate a colleague's paper is difficult to do. A good way to initiate this culture is for the senior members of staff to go first and illustrate humbleness that enables open and unconstrained debate and the creation of new and different ideas of phrasing a research problem. Respectful engagement is key here, so that other members of a department recognise that there is so much to gain from such an in-depth debate and that any fears of excessive negative criticism and undermining are unfounded.

47. Keep up with current affairs

Ideas spawn from a variety of places, including from our peers in open, constructive and opportune conversation, but one area that we should nurture and regularly engage as a source of knowledge is current affairs. The real world is the best model of itself and lessons reveal themselves through examples to interpret, perspectives to recognise and disagreements to appreciate.

 Contextualising your research within current affairs enables you to emphasise the relevance of your own research to your readers. This will strengthen the perception of validity of your research and it will encourage your readers to appreciate the differences between contexts, cultures, attitudes, values and beliefs. You can use your knowledge of current affairs to highlight why social differences occur, the importance of path dependency and the significance of peer effects and social norms in making decisions and shaping policy.

> Men make their own history, but they do not make it as they please; they do not make it under self-selected circumstances, but under circumstances existing already, given and transmitted from the past. (Karl Marx, 1852)[1]

The diversity of opinions and interpretations of current affairs add to the rich tapestry of modern social sciences and can make us realise how much we can learn and how much we have progressed since the early writers in our own disciplines. All communications of news and current affairs will have a degree of reporting bias, and you can explicitly recognise this subjective narrative in your research, as it may allow you to question understanding, stances, policies and/or progress in the past, present and future. News and its narrative can break down or construct prejudices, and this is at the heart of social science research.

 Deep and broad knowledge of current affairs can impress your readers and audience, and it can heighten the validity of your research in their minds. Making these connections requires grounding in the real world, but many academics still focus their research on a hypothetical world of assumptions, over-abstraction and oversimplification. Although there is a place for both applied and theoretical activities, you will achieve greater impact when you can do both.

Newspapers and other news mediums can provide an abundance of anecdotal evidence that you can cite to contextualise your social science research.
Transferring your understanding of current news stories to your readers in the
form of contextualised strengths, weaknesses, opportunities and threats can
augment the perceived power of your work and strengthen the contemporary
case for the adoption of a particular theoretical perspective or policy.

Research leaders should be highly engaged with the real
world. Knowledge of contemporary affairs enables them to
probe and question their own and their colleagues' work to
ensure that the relevance of their research is developed to
its fullest extent. By encouraging colleagues to contextualise
and engage with current affairs, research leaders can inspire their colleagues
to make increasingly pertinent research contributions to today's literature,
society and policymakers' actions.

Embedding current affairs and contexts into research outputs takes practice.
Although formal training is probably unwarranted, regular examples and discussions of current affairs and how they relate to different colleagues' research
programmes should be actively encouraged by those leading research within
a department. Once this is embedded as good practice, you will be surprised
how frequently your colleagues approach each other with snippets of current
affairs that may be relevant to their work and which they may have missed.

NOTE

1.   Marx, K. (1852), *The Eighteenth Brumaire of Louis Bonaparte*, Die Revolution.

48. Participate actively in staff seminars

Presenting research in front of one's own department can be more daunting than presenting in front of a large international audience. One reason for this is that you think that you will never hear the last of it if you make a mistake, so you put added pressure on yourself.

Try to use this fear positively by strengthening your presentation skills so that you are clearly humble and visibly wish for constructive criticism, because in the end that feedback will help you. Not participating actively in staff seminars will only diminish your own speed of research and delay receipt of the feedback that you require to progress.

Irrespective of how your staff seminar actually goes, make sure you show a serious and strong appreciation for your colleagues' time and questioning: that appreciation should come across in a way that illustrates your gratefulness for their efforts to constructively criticise your work. Ensure that you recognise that you have benefited from their insights.

 Active participation in your department's staff seminars creates benefits in two mains ways. First, present your own work and you will receive useful feedback and, second, you can provide insightful feedback to your colleagues on their work.

If you are facing a particular obstacle in your research, then underline that obstacle in your presentation, as someone in your audience may be able to solve it for you relatively easily and save you a huge amount of time. Strongly encourage comments from the audience by saying things like "I'm finding this a bit difficult, any ideas please?"

Members of the audience want to know your research contributions, not someone else's, so do not spend most of your allocated time outlining the existing literature; instead, only refer to the literature to underscore the gap that you are trying to fill. You will be unable to remember all of the questions and points from the audience, so bring with you a notebook and a pen and actively write down their comments as the seminar proceeds; this shows that you are treating their thoughts seriously and that could encourage them to comment further, thereby helping you even more.

Present your research as often as you can. Present it internally initially, whenever you think that it is ready for feedback, and present it externally to gain potentially a very different set of comments from diverse perspectives.

Internal presentations are best for undeveloped research papers, but never present a finished paper in staff seminars, as doing so would frustrate your audience that they are unable to help you on your research journey. Simply presenting research that is in its final polished stage will bring audience members less satisfaction because you will be giving them fewer opportunities to interact and think laterally.

Of course, if you are trying to impress an external audience in the hope that you will get a job in the institution that you are visiting, then it is better to present a paper that is closer to completion, but in these circumstances it is still best to show potential areas of overlap and value-added.

Present whenever you need an incentive to complete a research manuscript, as it can be the motivation that you need to achieve this aim.

Research leaders should frequently present in their own department staff seminars. Research leaders have a crucially important role here for several reasons: first, they need to prioritise attending every session to be an example to their colleagues of the importance of attendance. Second, they should illustrate to others the acceptable questioning phraseology: constructively critical and helpful without belittling or undermining.[1]

Third, research leaders must talk to specific colleagues on a one-to-one basis afterwards if they are using condescending, belittling or undermining language to a speaker, and highlight that this is not acceptable and show them examples of alternative, less condescending ways to express concerns they may have about their colleagues' research. It is up to research leaders to model, emphasise and illustrate what language and behaviour is expected of their colleagues.

Research leaders should ensure that their colleagues feel safe when presenting their research, without fear of condemnation. Research seminar atmospheres that are confrontational will reduce the incentive and willingness to present, and in turn this will reduce the pace and quality of research undertaken by colleagues, simply because they will avoid those opportunities to gather feedback.

NOTE

1. Those who phrase their points and questions in a condescending and belittling way are often doing so because of their need to appear bigger than they feel. If you do receive such questioning, be conscious that their phraseology is unlikely to be because of something that you have done, but rather that it is a reflection of their feelings towards themselves.

49. Organise your department's staff seminar series

A staff seminar series can and should act as the nexus for the departmental discussion of all things research related. It can be the pinnacle of the working week whereby researchers across topics (though typically within a department) congregate to inspire and to be inspired to think about a specific research issue.

The stresses and strains of organising such a vital part of the week cannot be trivialised, but it is also an easy and enjoyable role to undertake if done properly and collaboratively. This is where you can make your name as an externally connected researcher and make a vitally important contribution to the research culture and atmosphere within your department.

This role is ideal for a mid-career researcher and can work best when there are two colleagues working together effectively. The role enables a colleague to initiate, strengthen existing or make more and new connections, locally, regionally, nationally or globally for themselves, for their department, and for their university. Organisation of a staff seminar series gives you the opportunity to expand the academic networks of everyone within the department, hence the reason why this role is so crucial for the long-term vitality of a department.

Initiation or reinvigoration of a staff seminar series has a host of challenges. When a department does not fully embrace such a series, the memories of old seminars could be of a parochial session on a topic of distant interest that you were coerced to attend to make up audience numbers. Instead of experiencing the session as an instrumental opportunity to expand lateral thinking and cogitate on rewarding content, it can transform into a ceremonial duty to depict to the external speaker or senior internal colleagues that you and the rest of the department are engaged, and to expose the department to the external speaker as an interesting and rewarding place to work. Although an external visibility of engaged and interested research is vital, this is much more convincing if it is natural and honest behaviour rather than if it is coerced.

In my opinion, organisation of the staff seminar series is one of the most important roles within a department. When a staff seminar series has a vibrant, open, respectful and energising atmosphere, it can bring colleagues together from within and beyond a department, act as a nexus between different colleagues' research identities, set the atmosphere for research engagement and reflection, excite and inspire colleagues, and break down real and imagined barriers between colleagues. It also displays to prospective applicants that the department is a good place to work.

Staff seminars must be regular, collegiate, collaborative, accessible, non-confrontational, rewarding, enjoyable, supportive and critically constructive sessions that all colleagues look forward to as a highlight of their working week. If any of these attributes are not present, someone needs to grasp the initiative and make that change. Sometimes it will be down to the organisers themselves, and including tea, coffee and cakes, etc. can break any formalities. If a colleague is confrontational and disruptive or too dismissive, then action should be taken by a senior colleague to pull that colleague to one side and have a quiet word to encourage them to change their tone without reducing their engagement. Speakers' topics need to be relevant and interesting for colleagues across the department, so the latter should be empowered to suggest potential speakers. The organiser can, therefore, be the engaged academic administrator of the series, but the success of the series depends on the contributions of all colleagues in the department.

 The research leader should allocate the role of staff seminar organiser to someone who cares passionately about research and the development of the department. Clearly, someone who has a low level of engagement, does not communicate with their internal colleagues enough on research matters, has a limited external network or may represent your department in anything other than the best light is not the ideal candidate for this role.

The staff seminar organiser role should be rotated proactively across the department, so that all appropriate colleagues can benefit individually and collectively. One way to rotate this role is to ask a new appointee to shadow the outgoing post-holder for a year, ask them to undertake the role for a full year or two on their own, and then identify a new appointee to shadow them in order to learn the role.

Research leaders need to ask their contacts in other universities to come and present, which invariably they accept. Research leaders should also make sure that the staff seminar organiser receives enough support in this strategically important role, because some less experienced researchers with small networks may face difficulties attracting speakers and be too embarrassed to ask for help.

50. Organise workshops

If you have lots of experience running a staff seminar series, the next stage of your development may well be to organise a half-day workshop on a theme that you wish to be known for. You should think judiciously about how many delegates you wish to congregate in the room and the breadth and depth of discussion. For instance, if your area of research is local development, then you will want to have senior and early career scholars working on this area to attend the workshop. You may also wish to engage specific groups of non-academic stakeholders and must consider whether you wish to include only local non-academic stakeholders or whether you wish to invite national representatives too. How far you engage with non-academic groups will depend on your current and expected future contacts and the extent of your desire and ability to engage in impactful research.

There needs to be clear value added for the presenters and members of the audience. You may wish to encourage councillors to present something that they wish to solve or get feedback on. You may ask for representatives of groups of people whose opinions and needs matter most for the topic, such as residents. You could ask companies who invest in the area about the factors that attracted them to the area, and details on what could be improved. You could engage with career services to identify why some local graduates do not consider remaining in the area. You could engage with large local businesses to try to identify the skills they would like their students to possess on graduation that may be missing.

Your engagement with the non-academic community can be as wide and as deep as you wish to make it, and a workshop can put your name on the map if it is successful. Excluding a particular group, such as local residents in the example above, could enhance the focus of your academic research or reduce its relevance and applied nature. In other words, these decisions can be unexpectedly beneficial, a calculated risk or a mistake. People will remember you for the relative success of this initiative, with greater success bringing greater attention, opportunities and benefits to your career, department and university.

Time is precious for academics, policymakers and for all your attendees. Make sure that your workshop has a very clear focus and that you are the academic that delegates are likely to think of and recognise as being prominent in that specific research area. However, before you embark on such a major project, you need to establish your name around the topic first, and this is likely to require several substantively important already-published journal articles.

An alternative strategy is to organise a workshop on a topic that is far from your own research area but on a topic that is of substantial current and pertinent interest to the university's catchment area. Here your role would be to bring together individuals to discuss the topic. In this case, you will become known as a facilitator and organiser of workshops on pertinent topics with connections that can bring stakeholders together.

 Research leaders should run workshops on a semi-regular basis and use them as an illustration of best practice to less experienced colleagues. They should include colleagues interested in the running of workshops, so that they too can learn the challenges of setting up and running them.

Research leaders could suggest the idea of running a workshop to colleagues when they recognise that they are uncovering something important that could benefit from discussion in a workshop format. They can help by encouraging colleagues from other universities to join in, and they could help to attract a keynote speaker.

PART VI

Conferences

There are many benefits of attending conferences. These include receiving feedback on your research, providing feedback to others to help improve their research, expanding your networks, updating your knowledge of the areas of research that are trending at a point in time and becoming known on the academic circuit.

All of these benefits will be woven into the tips in this section, but the most important reason to attend conference is to make time for inspiration, networking and feedback. Below are tips for good practice that aim to maximise the levels of feedback, networking and inspiration that you will receive from conferences.

51. Planning conference attendance

Make sure that you attend the most beneficial conferences. You are likely to have a limited conference budget, so you need to balance quality and quantity. Prioritise the most suitable type of conference for the stage of your career. The most appropriate conference for you and your attendance frequency will evolve with experience.

Your knowledge of the skills, expertise and research interests of other delegates will evolve too. You will communicate regularly with some of those delegates face-to-face at conferences. If you make the effort to network well then you will get to know others well enough to phone them for a chat and to pick their brains even though you may not attend the same conference for several years. These networks are incredibly important.

You will want to attend some conferences for instrumental reasons, because presenting at them enables you to receive constructive and informative feedback on your research. You may want to attend other conferences to show that you are conforming to the wider discipline, whether you present at them or not. Attendance at some conferences is expected within some disciplines. You may want to attend other conferences in order to learn something new or from a different perspective, such as when an economist attends a sociological conference, and vice versa.

Some conferences have more beneficial effects than others. The type of benefit will also vary, depending on what you are setting out to achieve. If you are aiming to receive (and offer) appropriate feedback, you will want to attend a field conference that is specifically focused on your research area. If you are looking for a new job, you may want to attend a conference that is core to the discipline. If you wish to expand your networks in order to recruit and expand a team on a grant application, you will want to attend a conference that includes specific delegates. Be strategic with your conference funds and spend them wisely.

Identify a priority for the stage in your career. A mid-career academic should attend a wider range of conferences to strengthen the breadth of their knowledge. Someone wishing to switch universities should attend ceremonial conferences. Anyone who has a piece of research on which they wish to have high-quality focused feedback should prioritise presentation of that research at a field conference.

Identify what you need most this academic year: is it feedback, greater breadth or ceremonial conformity that matters? Sometimes you will want to become known and strengthen others' knowledge of you, so appearing at that conference may ensure that you are at the forefront of others' considerations when, for instance, they wish to put forward a grant application and when they are looking for someone with your skills. Becoming known for your strengths is key for your future progression.

 Research leaders should know their colleagues and conferences well enough to be able to help colleagues identify which type of conference they should attend. They can provide guidance and sometimes assistance in ensuring that junior researchers submit an abstract before a deadline. Research leaders should also highlight the need to prioritise particular conferences within budgetary constraints.

One of my first research leaders – Marion Jackson – was instrumental in identifying the right conference for my research. She recommended that I attend a conference that I had not heard of, and I have been a regular delegate on that conference circuit ever since. Apparently, it took her years to find the conference for her own research, and was so pleased with it that she had the enthusiasm to pass this knowledge on to me and, of course, I will always be thankful for that informed and excellent guidance.

52. Listen properly to questions from the audience

When you wish to gain feedback on a research topic that you are finding challenging, it is very easy to become nervous and tense and rush through the content of your presentation. Many delegates may see this as simply poor presentation skills, and they may find it frustrating. In this situation it is common for presenters to desire the session to pass quickly, resulting in nerves that are so highly strung that the presenter does not listen to the questions from the audience effectively enough and misses the opportunity to learn something potentially very insightful from the audience.

Very poor practice was evident to me at a prestigious conference several years ago. In response to a delegate's question, the high-profile and well-known presenter simply responded by saying, "well, that is already established in the literature". The delegate asked a valid and insightful question, but it was astounding to several delegates in the room how fixed to the literature the presenter was, rather than being embedded in the real world. Although the question was asked clearly, the presenter either did not listen to the question properly or chose to ignore the content of that question, and either excuse reflects rude behaviour to the delegate who bothered to ask the question, and the audience in general.

When you are presenting, make sure that you realise that the vast majority of people asking you questions are there to provide you with their best constructive feedback. The second type of questioning is when a delegate has been inspired to ask a question for clarification or to encourage you to go further. These types of question could eventually be a section within the published version of the paper.

Challenging and new topics will stimulate a huge amount of interest and debate, and many questions can follow. If you do not answer questions appropriately, the individuals asking them will feel as though you have ignored them. This is very poor practice, and something that you do not wish to be remembered for.

There are two main types of questions that a presenter will receive from the floor. Unfortunately, there are on occasion some audience members who have a need to belittle other presenters. Under these circumstances, it is natural for presenters to try to identify whether the questioning is a social threat in front of their peers. If it is an attempt to undermine you as a person, the best thing is to show others in the audience that you can rise above it. Thank the delegate for their time in asking the question, even write the issues down to reflect on constructively at a later time, and then move on to a question from someone else. People in the audience will be impressed by your ability to park the personal attack, and this can actually alienate the arrogant person asking the question, in which case you won that battle!

Try to listen for the difference between these two types of questions, because how you listen and respond can significantly affect the rate at which you learn and develop your work. Quickly park the obnoxious delegate's question and move on to the well-intentioned, inspirational and genuinely interested audience member's question. The latter type of delegate may even share a coffee with you afterwards.

 Once you have identified the intentions of the person asking the question, make sure that you fully understand the question being asked. If you do not understand the question, or if you need more time to think about the answer, then ask them to repeat the question or rephrase the question in your own words to ensure that you understand the question. This response is perfectly acceptable, and much better than providing an answer to a question that was not asked.

An alternative approach is to provide an answer and then ask the questioner whether they thought the answer you gave was sufficient to answer their question. If you do this in a polite and accommodating way, then they may put in further effort to explore the issue more. Often, they will reflect on your answer and suggest that the two of you discuss the point after the session, which is great as someone is interested enough to engage with your work out of a session.

Make sure you thank everyone individually for asking questions; they did not have to! Listen as much as you can to others' presentations, recognise how others ask questions and make sure that you are at least as approachable as the most approachable questioner. Do not be the fountain of all knowledge when presenting at a conference (you will come across as arrogant), and admit that you do not know something if you are unsure how to answer their question; it is much better coming across as an informed individual who is willing to learn more than pretending that you know everything already.

 Research leaders need to be humble and honest about the breadth and depth of their knowledge. All good academics know that despite everything we know there is so much more that we do not know, not least those questions that are 'unknown unknowns'. The best academics know that much knowledge is built on fragile assumptions that need to be unpicked and assessed in greater depth.

Conferences, and staff seminars for that matter, are not an opportunity to showcase how wonderful and intelligent someone is; they are opportunities to push knowledge forwards. Development of a collegiate, enquiring, yet humble culture will ensure greater knowledge accumulation and faster momentum towards better understanding.

53. Attend as many conference sessions as you can

When you attend a conference, do not waste your precious time by working on your own research when someone else is on stage; this is your opportunity to learn from the speaker! Yes, you may have pressing engagements and deadlines to meet, but you must rearrange them so that you can devote your time and fullest attention to listening to and learning from others.

 Conferences are usually a dynamic and stimulating arena of contrasting approaches, ideas and wayward thoughts that stimulate lateral thinking and mind-bending policy-related questions. Listening to others' ideas stimulates your own thinking and often creates connections between points that you may not have made otherwise. Creative ideas and talks that challenge philosophies, opinions and, potentially, even universally accepted concepts open minds and lead us to question what we think we know.

Conferences challenge your current thinking patterns, and stimulate your interest to move to new, undiscovered ideas that demand cogitation. Those ideas can distract you and/or nuance your own research so that you become more specific and attune to the newest ideas. This rumination and stimulation is why you entered academia, so enjoy it to its fullest and participate actively in as many relevant conferences as you can.

 Skip conference sessions and you forego these stimulating opportunities. Attend as many potentially interesting conference sessions as you can. There will be time for your own research later, you do not know what and when that gem of insight or spark of an idea will come your way, and missing stimulating conference sessions will reduce the frequency and probability that ideas will come your way. You can work on your own research after the presentations and social activities.

 Intellectual heavyweights in many academic disciplines rarely skip relevant conference sessions because they recognise that they are opportunities to keep up with the literature, identify new talent (who are potential future colleagues) and continue to give their insight and intuition to the next generation of academics. The best research leaders attend sessions by junior academics to provide them with support and to show interest in their work too, especially when alternative sessions appear of middle-ranking importance.

54. The importance of attending social events

Attend conference social events to make the most of these networking opportunities, even if you are shy. Avoid overconsuming alcohol. Try not to dominate conversations and do mix; don't be a wallflower. Be present and in the moment at all social events.

 Social events are potential opportunities to find out whom you could work with and who you should avoid working with. Obviously, a connection point between conference delegates at social events is a common research interest, and this can be where conversation starts. Sometimes conversations start with "I saw you present today, it was a good presentation" and proceeds to "do you think the same method of analysis can be applied to ..." or "you may need to reconsider issue X because in context Y the effect may be dominated by issue Z". Discussion then follows and sometimes the fact that you are not on stage presenting your ideas can mean that you are more amenable and responsive to others' thoughts and questions. These conversations can be dynamic and responsive, taking your academic ideas to their intellectual frontier. They can stimulate you to think in new ways, follow new exploratory paths or consider validity levels in different contexts.

Social events at conferences are often the spaces where new ideas are created, new co-authorships are formed, new grant applications are conceived and friendships born and strengthened. These friendships and working relationships can stay with you for the rest of your career, and those colleagues may be your future sounding boards when you need to know whether one of your new ideas makes sense.

 Sometimes you will be surprised who you bump into. I attended a conference in 1999 and, during the coffee break – also designed to be social – I filled a cup with hot water while making tea. A mature gentleman with an American accent joined my and did the same. We started talking, he was very convivial, but our conversation ended all too early, as the next session was called to start. I did not catch the gentleman's name but was impressed by his humbleness and approachability, and I was pleased by the gentleman's apparent interest in my work. The gentleman joined me in the next session, sat next to me in a sparsely populated room, and promptly fell asleep. He began to snore, quietly at first, but the volume began to rise. I gently nudged him to wake him up. He fell asleep again, closely followed by another snore and another nudge. We had a pleasant quick chat after that presentation, in which I apologised for waking him but explained why I thought it might be best, and it transpired that the gentleman had only flown into the UK that morning and was naturally jet-lagged. Then the next presentation was announced, and the presenter was a world-renowned professor whose work I had learnt about throughout my studies ever since my undergraduate days; it was to be a highlight of my working year to even in the same room as that speaker who I think should be a candidate for a Nobel Prize. Then the perfect gentleman sitting next to me, who I had earlier briefly shared a drink with and subsequently elbowed in the ribs, stood up and proceeded to walk to the stage. It just goes to show that the best academics can also be the most astonishingly approachable and convivial people.

Attend all social events at conferences, be they evening sessions, tours, coffee breaks, dinners or lunches. You never know whom you will meet and what you will learn.

 The best research leaders socialise effectively at conferences. They are approachable and are approached by a range of aspiring academics and other research leaders alike.

I recall a time early in my career when I wanted to return to my hotel room and finish off my presentation for the following day, but was convinced by a convivial research leader to attend a conference AGM. It was my first AGM and I thought that it would be a discussion of administrative and uninteresting duties; I was only partly correct. AGMs are also social settings, albeit relatively formal, that are packed full of research leaders. There you will find out who is a team player and wants to contribute to the greater good, and who may not be a team player. Never miss a social event.

55. Be yourself and enjoy conferences

As social animals, most of us enjoy interaction with fellow humans. However, if you are shy or reserved, try to put that behavioural tendency aside while at conferences. At conferences, you should assume that you are constantly on stage while recognising that you have something to offer the academic community and wider world. Consciously or subconsciously, other delegates will be making a judgement about whether you are a person they would like to work with, whether they can learn something from you, whether they should give you a job in the future, etc. Naturally, we gravitate to people who appear happy, are enjoying themselves, and have that infectious smile. Make sure you enjoy yourself at conferences and become known for the right reasons.

The best way to interact with colleagues at conferences is simply to be yourself. You will have already shown your ability during your academic studies and you have already (or will be about to) contribute to the literature. That contribution, however small, will be recognised by your peers. Of course, there will be many people who will have made contributions in areas where you will never be able to make substantive contributions, but that's because you will be researching slightly different areas – don't compare yourself to others.

There will be famous names who disappoint you, people you click with straight away and many other delegates who lie somewhere in between; this is all perfectly natural. At the same time, there is no reason to dominate conversation, as such individuals tend to be avoided by those delegates who simply want to take in the conference atmosphere without confrontation or overly strong debate.

Conferences are focused opportunities for the development of knowledge, and they are very effective if you immerse yourself in the intellectual and social atmosphere. Moynihan et al. (2015) go so far as to state that prosocial desire to help others is a basic human goal that matters to an individual's happiness.[1] So, as we learn more when we are engaged, and we are engaged more when we have higher levels of satisfaction, being yourself and enjoying yourself at conferences will enable you to get the most out of them and contribute the most to them.

Research leaders have an important role to play here too. First, they need to ensure that they are a positive example to others on how to interact at conferences. Second, they are there to pick up the pieces and support colleagues who need a confidence boost and a realisation of the importance and interest in their work. This includes providing moral support to those colleagues who have just been chewed up and spat out by a delegate whose questioning was unreasonably and unjustifiably aggressive.[2] Third, research leaders, especially the more respected ones, should have the competence to approach those unreasonably aggressive delegates and inform them that their behaviour is inappropriate. It is in the interests of the academic community that all colleagues, junior and senior, feel safe and welcome in our community so that they have the confidence to make a contribution to the literature. Research leaders in particular need to encourage constructive criticism in a humanistic and collegiate manner.

NOTES

1. Moynihan, D. P., DeLeire, T. and Enami, K. (2015), 'A life worth living: evidence on the relationship between prosocial values and happiness', *American Review of Public Administration*, 45(3), pp. 311–26.
2. Aggression is a moral evaluation that we make of other people's actions. See Sabini, J. and Silver, M. (1982), *Moralities of Everyday Life*, Oxford University Press.

56. Get known for something

Many of us have interests in a variety of research topics. We may start a paper and put it to one side while we pursue another idea. Sometimes we may even present an idea at a conference without the paper ever being published subsequently. However, once you have made a name for yourself on the conference circuit, delegates will attend your session to see what new ideas you are bringing to a specific research agenda, and they will form an impression about your current research trajectory. You will want to encourage those individuals to attend and provide you with constructively critical feedback and you will want to reward their attendance with information that they can take away with them and think over.

As you progress in your career, you must become increasingly known for something specific. This is important because those who wish to work with you need to know your strengths and may want to know how these strengths can be used in a team grant application.

This does not mean that you have to devote all of your efforts to the same specific research issue, as that can also illustrate your inflexibility in research. You may be asked to sit on grant funding panels, review papers for journals, chair conference sessions, or be a keynote speaker. People will need to know what you stand for, and that the quality of your work in an area is consistently good, so they know what to expect if they have you on their team. If you spread yourself too thin across research topics, your colleagues may not know what you excel at and may overlook you and ask someone else for help on an interesting research project.

Although following your research interests is a crucial way to remain engrossed in research, there may be times when you stray too far from a research area that others expect you to be researching. This is not a problem if it is clear to delegates that you are presenting something that is different to your usual research, but once I attended a conference where someone asked me of another presenter, "what is [individual X] doing presenting on that topic; he should return to something that he knows about". I was taken aback because 'individual X' was a well-known academic who published in some of the top journals. I was thinking "why shouldn't this person, or any other academic, pursue a research topic that they find interesting and feel that they could contribute to that literature?" On reflection, it appears that the individual questioning me was unable to appreciate the contribution that the famous presenter was making, and therefore they felt disappointed and underwhelmed by the academic who usually drew a large audience. Be aware that you may inadvertently disappoint some people if you present on a subject not in your usual research area.

 Knowing when the right time is to research something that is not your core area, simply to pursue an area of interest, remains tricky and difficult. There may be no right time for some, and there will always be more that we could achieve by maintaining focus on our immediate research topic. But being focused on one topic for many years can become monotonous and your research creativity could become stale. As long as you remain known for quality work in a particular research area then people will remember you, and thenceforth you will be able to spread your research wings and encompass a different research area to maintain your interest in research.

If you have not been able to stake a claim in an existing literature, or if your research output is not hitting the journals that you would like, maybe you need to make a contribution to the literature in a slightly different area, or you could work with someone who is already hitting those journals regularly. An alternative is to change your research area and focus on one that captures most of your interest.

 It is difficult for research leaders to provide guidance on this topic. Any such advice will inevitably challenge the individual's research identity and providing advice that challenges the researcher's perception of themselves can create unwanted friction.

Once I was working on an area that my research leader at the time was passionate about, but it was not one of my normal areas of research. That research leader advised me to drop the project and regain my research focus. But I didn't drop that project, and I eventually published the paper in a good journal. Part of the reason for my research leader's discouragement, in hindsight, might have been because I was encroaching on an area that he was trying to plough himself.

Therefore, a research leader should be encouraging a colleague to do the best at what they currently interested in, and perhaps help to identify gaps in knowledge that could be filled by that researcher. When a research leader expresses interest, support and enthusiasm for a colleague's research topic (irrespective of how closely their research aligns to the colleague's research), then the colleague will feel more supported and energised, and have the feeling that what they are doing is valued and important.

57. Display your contribution fully, but don't over-egg it

Have you ever been in a seminar when the presenter seems to push the importance of their work too strongly, and you simply do not see the apparent importance of their idea? Some presenters try too hard to make you appreciate a point. What works better is to draw the audience's attention towards and clearly highlight your research contribution, and then let them decide how important they perceive that contribution to be.

Do ensure that your research makes as much a contribution as possible and that the whole of the contribution is clear. Do not claim that you are making a vitally important contribution, because your audience will see straight through that claim. As long as you have outlined your contribution clearly enough, it is your audience who will decide whether your contribution is important. Unfortunately, if you claim that your contribution is vitally important, but your audience does not agree, you are more likely to be known for making *un*important contributions to the literature.

The best presentations and papers outline the gap in the literature along with the substantive contribution that would be made if that gap were filled. They underscore why the contribution is important, and then let the audience consider and reflect on whether your contribution fills that gap. Trying to pretend that you have reinvented the wheel will just make people think you did not fully understand the wheel in the first place. Failing to present the entire contribution is a missed opportunity to be recognised for making an important contribution to the literature.

Research leaders should encourage their colleagues to reveal their full research contributions, and this is a more usual problem than trying to rein in the over-emphasis of a contribution. Nevertheless, over-egging a contribution does occur, and this can be difficult to deal with for research leaders.

Good research leaders do not want to undermine their colleagues' contributions, and they want to encourage them to develop their ideas further, but trying to inform a colleague that their work is not as substantive or ground-breaking as they are making it out to be is often the wrong way to approach this issue; a better way to help colleagues improve the impact and importance of the research is to devote time to helping them develop their ideas even more.

58. Offer to present papers in other staff seminar series

When you find someone working on a research area that is close to your own, and if you have a lot of respect for them and their ideas, then a good way to encourage them to recognise your work too is to schedule in a date to present your work in their department's staff seminar series. It is surprising how few researchers participate in this circuit, especially given the high potential pay-offs.

 Presenting in another department's staff seminar series has many benefits:

1. Academics attending your session will be more aware of your research abilities and the contributions that you are making to the literature.
2. Those academics might be more likely to cite your work.
3. They may appreciate that you have skills that they do not have.
4. They may find you approachable and be someone that they could work with.
5. The presentation and subsequent discussion may stimulate new ideas for research. If the third, fourth and fifth points come together at once, there is the possibility that you will commence a new research project with a well-known and high-quality academic.
6. You will receive ideas that could push your research forward and these ideas will have come earlier than they would have if you did not present your research in the seminar series.
7. Preparation for the presentation may lead to you recognise a gap or an extra contribution that you may not have appreciated prior to your preparation.
8. This is an excellent way to increase the number and quality of colleagues within your academic network.
9. You could consider your presentation as an in-the-job-market presentation, because audience members will unconsciously (or consciously) be considering whether they would mind you being part of their department.
10. You may experience a degree of confrontation and support that will inform you whether you would be interested in working in that department.

You should aim to present at two external staff seminars per year. Ideally, these presentations will be in departments that have staff members whose research interests overlap with your own, as the more your research interests overlap the more focused questions that you will receive. Try to make sure these presentations are several weeks apart, especially if you will be presenting the same paper in both external seminars; in this way, you will have time to adjust your paper in line with the comments of the first seminar prior to the second seminar, and the feedback from the second seminar could further nuance those changes.

Undertaking fewer external presentations will reduce the feedback that you receive, whereas too many presentations will impinge on your other duties, such as teaching and administration, which could further push back the completion of your paper. Find the right balance for you, given your administrative and teaching workload, and work around those constraints if you need to.

 Research leaders should make suggestions to their less experienced colleagues of departments in other universities that have members who would have high levels of interest in their research paper. They should highlight to their colleagues the importance of receiving this feedback, and they should visibly illustrate to their colleagues that they present at other universities themselves.

59. Being a sounding board strengthens network connections

Most academics welcome constructive feedback on their papers prior to submission. If you have the time and the interest in someone else's research, offer to read their paper prior to submission. You could give the paper a proofread or conduct a pseudo-full referee review. Once done, they may return the favour.

 Offering to provide feedback on others' research strengthens the reciprocal relationship that you have with your colleagues. It breaks down barriers and reminds each other that we support each other's endeavours and encourage them to achieve their potential. Knowing that you can simply walk down the corridor and ask a question of a colleague who has some knowledge of the topic, and that they are willing to devote time to help you, can considerably increase the benefits of working in the office and will appreciably strengthen the positive spillovers between colleagues. It will quicken the pace of research within a department while enhancing both job satisfaction and the perception that the department is a progressive place to work.

In the current environment, where Covid-19 has shifted many academics' working practices to their own homes, the connection between colleagues has been weakened and the feeling of research support has reduced. However, those academics who had already established strong reciprocal networks, and remained open to colleagues communicating with them, switched to Skype, Zoom and equivalents. Unfortunately, the gap between those who had already established such networks and those who had not seems to be reflected in their own perceived pace of research. Those with strong networks transferred to the virtual environment relatively quickly and have not been as negatively impacted, but those academics with relatively weak networks have suffered through a lack of connection. Informal research networks are much more difficult to establish within a virtual environment.

 It is important to provide feedback in a timely manner by using a narrative that is constructively critical and supportive. If something needs to change in a colleague's paper, tell them as early as you can so that it can benefit them the most. Do not hold back in providing constructive criticism when you are the sounding board, because that is your role in this reciprocal relationship, but present your criticisms in a way that is supportive and helpful rather than undermining and destructive.

 Research leaders should be sounding boards on papers, but they should also provide feedback on presentation style. Making time to help less experienced colleagues not only increases their colleagues' confidence and improves their presentation style, it also improves others' perceptions of the quality of research carried out by junior members within the department.

Research leaders should be very mindful of the potentially lonely research journey in single-author papers, especially for those with weak network connections, and this seems to be heightened during the Covid-19 pandemic. Switching internal staff seminars to an online environment has supported researchers' morale during the pandemic, but if these at-distance meetings give less experienced staff members a feeling that everyone else is achieving at a faster rate than they are, they may become more anxious about their own pace of research and quality of research contributions.

Under such circumstances, research leaders need to be fully approachable and actively support all their colleagues, and be mindful of the connection between self-identity, research achievement and well-being. Research leaders should always have regular contact with all their colleagues to ensure that they feel connected and valued. Those who have strong networks and are valued sounding boards within their networks will view this as a natural occurrence.

60. Offer to contribute to organising relevant conferences

Being part of a conference organising committee can be very rewarding. Giving something back to the academic community is very satisfying and worthwhile in many unforeseen ways. Although contributing to the organisation of a large conference can be a daunting thought, and you may question and worry about what would happen if something goes wrong, invariably that coordination goes well, especially when you proceed with clear communication between colleagues. Conference organisation stimulates camaraderie and an active team naturally pulls together to make it a success.

Being part of a team that runs an annual academic conference can be very rewarding indeed, especially when you are building your CV, and the experience will put you in the limelight. Other benefits of assisting in the running of a conference include your name on the brochure, mentions of your name in thank you speeches, regular communications between you and delegates, opportunities to widen your network and meet key academics, and often personal thanks directed specifically to you over coffee between sessions.

Helping to contribute to the organisation of a conference expands your networks and increases the recognition of your contribution to academia. It will provide you with extra skills or take those skills to a higher level, and these will prove to be very useful in subsequent initiatives, not least with regard to organisation skills, time management and dealing with difficult people. Without your voluntary contributions, some of these conferences will not go ahead, and that will be a loss to the academic community.

Those academics who strive to contribute to the speed of research in a specific sphere of the literature fully recognise the need to congregate to discuss topics in a constructively critical, broad, open, non-confrontational and accepting culture. This is particularly pertinent in face-to-face arenas that spawn the benefits of networking. There will always be a need for someone to organise these conferences.

You should be sure that you make a contribution to the association that has greatest relevance for your research identity, as the pay-offs from your contributions will be limited if you are not really part of that particular research community. Once you properly recognise your own research identity and the most relevant association for you, it is time to increase others' awareness of your contribution to that association, and that is the time for you to join their conference organising committee.

Stepping up to an organising committee is likely to occur only after several years of post-doctoral experience during which you may change the focus of your research. It is appropriate to step down three to five years later when the next generation of academics join the organisation and turn your attention to other projects. Much later, you may be asked to step up again and become the organisation's chairperson, and the honour that you receive simply from being asked to take on this highly visible and responsible role is a reflection of your continuous contribution to the literature and to the association itself.

 Research leaders will know how important these external roles are for the visibility of less experienced colleagues, and they should be aware when those colleagues have greater workloads to deal with when they also have those external organisational responsibilities. A good research leader will lighten the burden by undertaking roles that give their colleagues more space to develop their understanding of the external roles and responsibilities. For instance, the role of organising internal staff seminars is not the right role for someone with time consuming external roles; sometimes a reorganisation of internal administrative roles is required due to increases in external visibility and associated duties.

The co-location of an association's Chair and a conference organising committee member, such as the association's secretary, can be fruitful for the smooth running of the association and its conference. This co-location can naturally lead to an academic institution being the optimal place to host an annual conference, and a wider local organisation committee could then be created under the direction of the research leader.

PART VII

A journal loop: reviewing and submitting papers

Papers published in journals are supposed to be of the highest scholarly standards. To ensure that each paper reaches this standard there is a peer review of journal submissions, which highlights how the paper could be improved and makes a recommendation to the editorial staff about whether the paper is acceptable for publication in its current format. Reviewing submitted papers for journals is a vitally important part of the review system, and it allows you to help to propel research forward and contribute to the shaping of your specialised area of the wider literature.

When we read a paper, we interpret and understand it from our training background and the knowledge and experience that we have accrued along the way. Our knowledge and experience shape what we expect to read in a journal article, how readily we would accept the relaxation of particular explicit and implicit assumptions, whether we are open to radical alternative views and how resolutely steadfast we are to maintain a mainstream status quo.

This approach to ensuring quality in journal publications has many strengths, but it also has some weaknesses. The publication of papers in journals is socially informed and is the result of the interaction of demand and supply forces. An underlying dominant world view coupled with methodological expectations can result in the continuance of a perspective even when that perspective and knowledge is known by some to be out of date.

Accepting these limitations, journals are an indicator system of quality, and we currently do not have a better way of documenting the evolution of knowledge. Therefore, we have a duty to our disciplines to participate actively in ensuring that journals publish the highest quality papers possible and help to move forward our understanding of our world.

61. Rarely decline offers

Journals will contact you every now and then and invite you to review a journal submission. If you are able to provide them with a good quality, rigorous and informative referee report on the submission that presents an analysis of something that you are familiar with, then think very carefully before you turn down this opportunity. The editor will have spent a period of time thinking about who would be the most appropriate referees for that specific submission, so the editor already recognises you as an authority in that area of the literature.

 By agreeing to undertake a refereeing duty, you are agreeing to constructively criticise a piece of research that could be a cutting-edge contribution. It may be a fascinating article that you will be one of the first to read. The submission could contain information that allows you to remain ahead of the literature curve. It also allows you to suggest corrections to any errors. You would be missing out if you turned down this refereeing opportunity.

 I have only turned down the opportunity to review one paper. This arrived in my inbox immediately before a two-week holiday that was followed immediately by a job and family relocation to the other side of the world, which would include a house search and a settling in period to a new job. I did not want to let down the journal and the submitting author(s) by delaying the refereeing process and I was unable to guarantee that I would be able to write the review within a month or two. For family reasons, therefore, I had to turn down that refereeing opportunity. Unfortunately, ever since I turned down that single reviewing opportunity, that journal has not asked me to review any further papers for them, and this means that I am unable to keep ahead of the curve with papers published in that journal.

 Some less experienced staff may need guidance on writing a review for a journal. Research leaders will have a wealth of experience in this area and should be able to provide guidance when needed. Sometimes this guidance will be to confirm that the colleague is fair. At other times, there is the need to encourage greater constructive criticism, and sometimes there will be the need to encourage the reviewer to rein in expansive requests for changes, based on the research leader's judgement and experience. There may also be occasions when a journal asks a research leader to review yet another paper but that it may be appropriate for the research leader to turn down the opportunity and pass it on to a junior colleague to increase their experience of reviewing a paper for a journal.

62. Be critical and demanding when reviewing, but also courteous

When writing a review of someone else's submission, it is essential to keep a delicate balance between being constructively critical and being respectful. You need to identify areas for further work in order to help the author(s) make it the best article that it can be, but your criticism should never be condescending or patronising in any way. Your review should be helpful and provide direction irrespective of how good the paper actually is.

 If there is something wrong with the paper, you must inform the editor about the issue; after all, the role of the referee is to inform the editor whether the paper is good enough and ready for publication. Sometimes the proposed modifications will be trivial while others will be more significant. Fatal errors tend to occur because the author(s) of the paper was focusing on another aspect of the argument, because they did not appear to know particular relevant literature or because they were confounding opposing philosophical perspectives. A referee's role is to point out these gaps and errors, and provide enough information so that the editor will be able to make a judgement about whether they should entertain a resubmission, accept the submission or reject the paper completely.

You will receive some excellent papers to review, and it is tempting to recommend acceptance straight away; in some cases, this is entirely appropriate. However, editors will want your guidance on whether the paper could be improved further to enable it to achieve its fullest potential and maximise potential citations.

 Even though excellent papers are often submitted to journals, it is rarely the case that those papers are finished perfectly. In these circumstances, make sure that you highlight that it is an already excellent paper and that it could be improved further by doing X or Y. Phrased in a way that emphasises that these recommended changes may increase citations or impact etc., they should only be welcomed by the author.

Even when the paper is fatally flawed, do highlight to the author(s) how they can improve it to make it publishable. Stopping your review at a point where you identify why the paper is flawed is not helpful. Try to ensure that your feedback is constructive and useful, and enables the author to move knowledge on to the next stage.

 Research leaders can offer advice to less experienced staff to ensure that they are being both constructively critical and supportive to the author(s). Sometimes this guiding role will need to adjust the language to ensure that it is appropriate and supportive, whereas at other times there may be a need to encourage the rewriting of the review in order to enhance the level of constructive criticism.

I have assisted colleagues when they recognise that the paper is inappropriate for a journal; highlighting to the editor that the paper is distant from what their readership would expect (such as a purely empirical paper in a deeply theoretical journal) is both useful for the editor and for the author(s) of the paper, as both will want to maximise their readership.

63. Have the cheek to ask difficult questions

Sometimes you will recognise a gap in the argument that really needs to be filled. It may be a difficult improvement to make, and hence the author of the submission may have tried to steer the paper away from you thinking about that issue. Nevertheless, if you think that a paper needs a slight refocusing, you should highlight it seriously to the editor. Sometimes the most difficult things to achieve are also the most important. If this is the case, although the author(s) may be frustrated in the short run, if your recommendation generates a much better paper, with a higher number of readers and a greater number of citations, the amended or enhanced issues are in the interests of both the author(s) and the editor.

 As a referee, you have the right to state your professional and constructive opinion on the submission to the editor. If you emphasise the need for the author to do something difficult, then you also need to state whether this is, in your opinion, a crucial aspect of the paper or whether this is simply desirable.

Even if you state that this is only a desirable point, the suggestion of the difficult issue will raise its attention in the minds of the authors, and this could push the literature forward in either that specific paper or a future paper perhaps by the same author(s). After all, your allegiance is to the search for greater understanding.

 Passive referees do not push the literature forward enough; active ones do. As long as a paper is viewed on its merits, and as long as suggestions for improvement are constructively critical and well meaning, so the editor can make the decision based on your recommendations about what revisions, if any, are needed for resubmission. Authors need suggestions for improvements in their paper, and referees are there to assist in this process.

 Some less experienced staff may not be as critical in their reviews of papers as they could be. Encouraging them to be more critical is a role for the research leader, and often this can be done very effectively during a chat over coffee. By developing a constructively critical and supportive atmosphere in their department, senior research staff can nurture an atmosphere that facilitates challenging questions and stimulates deeper thought, often to the benefit of less experienced colleagues.

64. Decline offers to review a paper if you would be a poor reviewer

Notwithstanding tip #61, there are few things more frustrating in academia than waiting for a referee report from a journal and finally, after a long wait, receiving it and realising that the referee has very little, if any, understanding of the relevant literature. Recently I received precisely that, so I passed the report on to a professorial colleague who knew my work well, to try to identify if I was missing something; my colleague's response was:

> The referee clearly doesn't understand some very basic things ...

I was embarrassed (as was my professorial colleague) that the journal even considered the referee report, as the points made were so misguided. Nevertheless, given the volume of papers now submitted to journals, it seems inevitable that this may occur from time to time.

If you accept a request from a journal to review a paper but realise subsequently that it is something that you know very little about, inform the journal as soon as you can, apologise to the editor that you don't have the skills to provide an effective review of the paper and then ask them to reallocate it to a different referee.

 The process of reviewing for journals is voluntary and necessary in order for the journal to reach a decision on whether the paper should be accepted for publication. The purpose of the referee report is therefore to guide the editor in making the decision. Editors regularly receive confidential feedback from authors, and they do recognise the weaknesses of particular referees. Referee reputations spread, and it would be surprising if this reputation does not also shape perceptions of paper submissions. At the other extreme, excellent referees receive prizes (such as the Emerald Literati Award). Your own reputation is at risk, so make sure that your referee report reflects well on your own expertise.

 It is always a good idea to write referee reports for journals, but you really need to make sure that your report is not only fair but also constructive in a way that builds on and expands the literature. You need to be able to justify properly your recommendation to the editor.

Conflicts of interest do occur, especially when you think you know the author(s) of the submitted paper. If that is the case, and it can happen frequently, then you need to be honest with yourself and make a value judgement about whether your report will suffer from either positive or negative bias. If either of these occurs, you should try your hardest avoid it and if you cannot, for whatever reason, then the literature and our search for improvements in understanding will inevitably experience a setback; you owe it to the profession not to do this. When you turn down this refereeing opportunity, it can be good practice to suggest to the editor the name of an alternative reviewer.

 Research leaders will be well versed in writing referee reports for journals. They will be able to guide their less experienced colleagues on the ethical rights and wrongs involved in writing such reports.

65. Learn from the papers that you review

Treat the opportunity of reviewing a paper as a chance to really dissect and understand what someone else is researching. There may be errors in that paper, but there may also be a strong rationale to adopt that approach instead of an alternative, standard perspective. Understanding *why* this was done puts you ahead of other researchers and enables you to enhance the depth and quality of your own research.

Sometimes reviewers undertake the task of reviewing a paper without recognising that this is also a learning opportunity for themselves. The paper should be a new potential contribution to the literature and could be important and insightful. Luckily, you have been given the opportunity to see it before most other people.

Use this opportunity to learn (and check) what you may have not fully understood before, such as a particular methodological technique or a particular philosophical angle. This opportunity can spark you into thinking about your own research in a different way. Often you will generate new ideas as you review other submitted (and published) papers, and always write down those new ideas of yours, articulate them enough to ensure that there is enough information to build on and save them for later when you return to your own research after writing the review.

Use all reviewing instances as opportunities to constructively criticise the author(s)'s work and to learn something new from the experience, however big or small. The author(s) should also learn from your ideas. And sharing these ideas through an anonymous referee report is a must, because it might push our literature forward.

There will be times when less experienced colleagues approach their research leaders for critical insight into the meaning and appropriateness of a particular statistical test in a paper they are reviewing, or of the relevance and appropriateness of adopting a particular theoretical or ontological perspective in a paper. Research leaders should support their colleagues by making time available to discuss these issues in the required depth. An in-depth discussion of a philosophical point can be not only engaging but also very enjoyable to both individuals.

66. Become known to the editorial team of a relevant journal

Once you have written a sufficient amount of notable published journal articles, it is good practice to ensure that you make yourself known to the editorial staff of the journals that you wish to be associated with most. This is unlikely to result in you being co-opted to the editorial staff straight away, but it is possible that they speak of you and your work in a positive way.

Being known to an editorial board can result in several benefits. One is that they may trust you to provide quality referee reports on areas that are close to your own research area, and this puts you at an advantage in being closer to the coalface of knowledge creation by others. Keeping abreast with the literature in your area is, after all, vital if you are going to push knowledge forward.

If those editors recognise your timely and thoughtful completion of referee reports, and if you emphasise that you would be prepared to provide more of them, they may take you up on your offer, which can be seen in a very positive light, especially when journal editors find referee reports delayed, slow and difficult to acquire. Being recognised as a person who contributes to academe can also cement people's respect for you as a team player. Being known and respected by the editors of a journal may also make them more open to being approached with ideas for special issues.

Once you have identified the specific area of the literature that interests you most, make sure that you make yourself known to the editorial staff of the journal(s) that you are interested in reviewing papers for. It may be that you have not yet published in that journal, but you intend to do so.

Most journals are always looking for more quality reviewers, and the proactive offering of your services will only ever be seen in a positive light. Perhaps the next paper that you review for them changes your research stance for the better forever!

If a research leader recognises that one of their colleagues is producing some excellent work in a particular literature, then they should mention it to their relevant journal contacts and encourage the editors to source appropriate reviews from the colleague, as this could be a good way for the colleague to keep abreast of the literature. The research leader could suggest to the editor that the colleague presents a paper in their university's staff seminar series so that they can judge the colleague's knowledge for themselves.

67. Appreciate that each journal focuses on something distinct

Often, we can be over-eager to submit a paper to a journal. Perhaps we are bored with constantly revising and polishing it, or perhaps our interests have already moved on to the next stage of developing the idea. Submitting a paper before it has been properly finished, and that includes shaping the narrative so that it conforms closely to the target journal's narrative, should be avoided at all costs, as it wastes huge amounts of time with the journal.

Each journal has its own narrative, represents a distinct set of world views and provides a particular type of literature to its readership. Each journal has its own groove, and if your paper does not fit that groove, it will be rejected. Your paper needs to ensure that it is written from the ideological perspective that concurs with the ideological perspective (and aims) of the journal's current editorial staff.

Consider your submission as an offer at a market. Consumers of your papers will prefer to purchase something that they consider to be most appropriate for their needs, and that means that you need to convince them that they need to buy your paper;[1] simply expecting a reviewer to recognise the quality of your work unfortunately will not be enough.

 Editors and editorial staff passionately believe in the vital role of their journal and that their journal, no matter which one it is and how highly it is ranked, has a crucial role to play in the evolution of their favoured literature. A journal reflects the editors' research identity and their priorities, and for some editors this means that their journal reflects a particular ideological perception too.

The important thing to remember is that most journal web pages will not reveal this information explicitly, and it may not be captured fully in the journal's name either. Instead, it is the responsibility of an experienced researcher to know their way around the journal market.

However, changes in editorial committees, which can happen every four or five years, naturally bring in slightly different perspectives and priorities. Just because a paper on a particular topic appeared in the journal four or so years ago (remember the time gap between initial submission and finally being in print) does not mean that the current editorial staff would be open to publish your paper on the same topic. It is naïve to think that a journal with, say, 'Regional' in the journal title would instantly be an appropriate journal to submit a paper that contains a particular geographical slant.

 Spend time getting to know your journals. Read the papers that interest you most and recognise when and where they were published. If you wish to contribute to that literature, the best place to get that paper published is in the same journal where you have read (and are citing) those papers.

This is one of the main problems with submitting papers to higher ranked journals; they may simply be inappropriate and you may be wasting your time by targeting a paper at a journal simply because it is rated higher on a particular metric.

If you wish your paper to be published in a higher ranked journal, you need to ensure that you use a narrative that is used in that journal. Editors do not have time to read and reread paper submissions, especially when some receive hundreds per year. If the paper does not immediately capture the editor's interest (i.e. be explicitly related to their journal's aims, philosophy, ontology, epistemology, etc.), it will be rejected no matter how technical, generalisable and wonderful you think that paper is. Senior researchers will also hear from their senior networks that a particular perspective is strengthening or weakening, and this knowledge could be of benefit to internal colleagues and co-authors alike.

Research leaders should keep abreast of the evolution of journals' aims and the evolution of journals' editorial staff, so that they are ready to highlight these changes to their colleagues where relevant.

NOTE

1. You could even consider whether the market for journal articles is an instituted myth. See Dugger, W. (1989), 'Instituted process and enabling myth: the two faces of the market', *Journal of Economic Issues*, 23(2), pp. 607–15.

68. Recognise the importance of the flow in arguments

Different journals publish papers with different flows of arguments; at one extreme you may encounter a detailed, philosophical and deliberative long narrative, while at the other extreme they may publish short sentences packed with descriptive numbers and shorthand equations. This may be due to the expertise of the authors, the journal's requirements for the structure of arguments, the topic and sometimes all three of these.

It is vital that you recognise these types of variations between journals and you must conform to the journal's style and expectation when submitting your paper. The degree to which you conform to their style and flow will significantly affect the probability of acceptance of your paper.

Your paper needs to be polished in a way that will appeal to the assigned editor and the editor-in-chief of the journal. If you simply and instantly submit a paper that was rejected by another journal without reformatting it to the style and expectations of the next journal, there is a very good chance that the paper will not be deemed good enough for the editor to distribute it to its time-scarce referees, and the paper will be desk rejected.

If the paper is sent to referees and even if you fulfil fully all of their demands, if the editor-in-chief (whose decision it is ultimately to accept or reject your paper) does not like how it reads, they will still reject it. Editors have this freedom and right, especially as many are inundated with submissions.

Every time you have a paper that is rejected, it is essential to avoid simply sending it off to the next journal down some journal rank. That new journal target may follow a completely different narrative and flow, which you must adopt explicitly if you think it is an appropriate outlet for your paper. If you believe that your paper is a good contribution to the literature and should be accepted regardless of the style and expectations, it will inevitably lead to your paper being rejected. The journal publishing game is like a market; you need to sell your paper to the editors and referees, and you can do that most effectively if you know their peer-informed preferences.

Research leaders should be very aware of the heterogeneous characteristics discussed above. They should offer assistance to their colleagues and be available to conduct a final read of papers prior to submission and/or resubmission. Less experienced colleagues should know that they can ask their research leaders for guidance and research leaders should actively encourage their approaches.

69. Try to review your own papers in the same critical way

A secret to writing excellent journal articles is having the ability to be as constructively critical about your own work as you are with papers that you review for journals. This not only requires the ability to engage critically with papers that you review for journals; it also requires the ability to transfer that critical engagement and reflection to evaluate and improve your own work. This is a very high-level, self-reflective skill and even the best academic authors usually rely on their networks to nudge their papers in the right direction, rather than relying on self-reflection alone.

 Sometimes your academic acquaintances may not have the time to review your papers and provide you with effective and constructive feedback. In these cases, you need to be able to rely on your own abilities to take your paper to the next level. This can be difficult for a number of reasons, such as perceptual blindness, where you will be unable to see unexpected issues purely because you have a lack of attention in that particular area. It is not possible to see all potential problems with your own work, as you will immerse yourself deeply in an issue and sometimes not see connected points. There will also be grammatical and spelling errors that we may not notice, because we often read what we think is written down rather than what is actually written down.

 Being constructively critical of others' work is difficult, but being constructively critical of your own work is twice as difficult. One tip is to complete your paper and then put it to one side and leave it alone long enough to not remember the exact phraseology of the text. The ability to step back and see your own work from a different perspective is improved with time-separation.

When I have been working on a script over many consecutive long days, I sometimes need a month between when I put the script to one side and when I pick it up again to edit it. This enables me to have a clearer critical eye and can help me move it along to the next stage.

Research leaders should be on hand to point out issues associated with perceptual blindness. They should respectfully highlight gaps in knowledge, omissions of thought and holes in arguments. Research leaders can encourage this self-reflection process by discussing the ideas with colleagues and encouraging them to think more critically and laterally. All colleagues will benefit from that focused attention, and research leaders could encourage them to engage in such activities between themselves. Make sure that this engagement is constructive and useful, and not a way of promoting one person over another; after all, the most important thing we are doing in this profession is advancing knowledge, and that should be the main focus of our engagements.

70. Submit your papers to the right journal

Each editorial team has their own ideas about the desirable direction of their journal. Editorial staff are very proud, and rightly so, about their own journal and genuinely wish to take their journal to the next stage in its development. It is paramount that you send your papers only to those journals that have editorial staff who will appreciate your perspective, as anything else will be desk rejected or waste your time.

 To avoid wasting your own and the journal editor's time, make sure that you situate your paper in literature that they know about. For example, if your paper presents an argument based on a world view that society can be viewed in terms of physics-like properties, reference to papers that present views that society is structured in institutions will not help your cause.

The majority of journals have their own ontology, epistemology, ideology and philosophy, and these may be explicit or implicit. Based on the relative importance of these issues to the current editorial staff, a journal's immediate future, and hence the papers that it will accept, will reside within these bounds. It is naïve to think anything else.

One of the most important ways to identify whether the journal is the correct outlet for your paper is to look at the list of references in your own paper and identity where those papers were published. If you are building on those papers – rather than simply dismissing them as having noteworthy problems – then the ideal journal target for your paper is likely to be the journal in which those key papers were published. Targeting your paper at the right journal, irrespective of its rank, is likely to result in the greatest chance of success.

 Know whether your target journal has recently changed its editorial board and/or focus. Understand the meanings behind the stated aims and scope of the journal. Get advice and openly discuss with your co-authors the likelihood of your paper being accepted by a journal and discuss the length of time that you are willing to wait for it to be published.

Ask for and gain advice about what other people think about the suitability of your paper for a journal. Targeting your paper at the wrong journal will simply add a delay, often six months, to the publication of your paper and, if your results are time-sensitive, this is not acceptable.

Compare your paper with those already published in the target journal. Note that the readers of that journal will expect papers similar to yours in past and future issues. Targeting the right journal also should enable you to leverage greater impact on the evolution of the literature than if you were to get it published with a journal that has a very broad remit. (Note also that this perspective undermines the relevance and importance of journal rankings.) Know your journals and continually update this knowledge.

 Research leaders should be open to questions about the right journal outlet for a colleague's paper (or even a paper that the colleague is refereeing). When reviewing colleagues' papers, always conclude by suggesting where you feel you would expect to read such a paper, and hence suggest a realistic journal target. Giving advice and openly discussing their perception of the likelihood of the paper being accepted in a particular journal, and adding a touch of realism to an author's perspective, may save the author time.

PART VIII

Teaching

Teaching duties dominate many of our working lives. The income that our universities receive directly or indirectly from students also pays for a large proportion of our wages. The key to being an effective and efficient research-focused lecturer is to ensure that there is a strong overlap between the content, structure, design and presentation of our teaching and research duties. For instance, it would be possible for a researcher of gender studies to teach issues in leadership and use a book that only covers issues relating to gender in passing, but it would be better, more effective, more inspirational, more insightful and probably more enjoyable for both the students and the lecturer if the context of the module included many issues relating to gender.

The benefits of synergies between teaching content and research interests are plentiful. Not only can students benefit from knowledge of the latest developments in the area, but they can also use their enthusiasm to bring the research content to life, not only about what we now know and what work is ongoing, but also about the gaps in knowledge that remain. Expressing complex ideas in a way that others can understand is also a challenge for researchers, and this need to increase the effectiveness of communication can require reflection and relearning of the ideas and active justification about why we approach a piece of research in a particular way. This can help the researcher question their own research and push their knowledge forward.

Studies such as Hattie and Marsh (1996) suggest that the relation between teaching and research is negligible.[1] It is also clear to see, simply by looking around a department, that the prioritisation of investigation over instruction is favoured by some (Flexner, 1930),[2] while the prioritisation of instruction over investigation is favoured by others (Barnett, 1992).[3] This focus and concentration also varies across universities, with some institutions specialising in research activities while others concentrate on teaching duties, and any separation can vary over time within departments and across a university. Notwithstanding this variation, this section highlights that there are many synergies between our teaching and research activities, and there are paths that can be followed to strengthen these synergies further.

NOTES

1. Hattie, J. and Marsh, H. W. (1996), 'The relationship between research and teaching: a meta-analysis', *Review of Educational Research*, 66(4), pp. 507–42.
2. Flexner, A. (1930), *Universities: American, English, German*, Oxford University Press.
3. Barnett, B. (1992), 'Teaching and research are inescapably incompatible', *Chronicle of Higher Education*, p. A40, available at https://www.chronicle.com/article/teaching-and-research-are-inescapably-incompatible/.

71. Teach a topic related to your research

Most academics are required to undertake both teaching and research duties. Depending on the balance of these two, and possibly other obligations, teaching-related duties can make up a large proportion of your time and energy at specific times of the academic year.

Given the amount of time that it takes to prepare and understand these pieces of knowledge in enough depth to be able to teach them effectively, you should attempt to ensure that you teach content that is related to your research. It is in your own and your institution's interest to have a strong alignment between your teaching and research duties in order to ensure the maximum amount of lecturer-led enthusiasm and inspiration.

 Many universities pride themselves on their research-led teaching, but if you are not researching the area that you teach, you are not contributing to this ethos. When you are not interested in the topics that you teach, your efforts in this area are likely to be lower than they could be, and therefore your ability to inspire and enthuse the next generation of academics will be reduced. When there is an excellent alignment between your research interests and your teaching duties, your energy and interest will arouse the imaginations of the students, thereby motivating them to also be interested in the topic and put in higher levels of effort to understand more fully the relationships of interest.

A further benefit of teaching an area that you research intensively is that you can bounce your ideas off the students in order to gauge their interest. Phrasing issues such as "the literature shows that we haven't yet solved the problem of …" or "in your dissertation you might wish to try to solve the problem that we currently do not know the answer to, that is …". Your inspired and energised students may one day be your postgraduate research student and solve that problem.

 Unfortunately, new appointees to a department will inevitably have to teach topics that are currently not being taught by existing members of staff. However, the longer you remain within an academic institution, the more modules that will become available for you to teach and, subject to a full suite of modules being covered, you will have the opportunity to switch between modules and teach topics that you are more comfortable with. Do let your Head of Department know about which modules you would like to teach in the near future, so that if that module comes availa-ble, and if the Head thinks it is a good change in teaching duties, you may well be offered that module.

 Research leaders should have an input into the teaching duties of a department's research staff. Many rankings of university departments also reflect research output, rather than simply teaching effectiveness and student feedback (which often reflects students' interest in the subject).[1] Not only will staff be more effective when teaching modules that reflect their own research areas, they will also be able to improve student evaluations through their infectious enthusiasm, thereby enhancing the satisfaction of students while increasing the job satisfaction of research-active lecturers.

Research leaders should therefore be able to recommend to the Head of Department prospective changes in the teaching duties for research-active staff. This discussion of recommended teaching duties may need to be handled sensitively to avoid some Heads of Departments thinking that the research leader is encroaching on their teaching-focused and administrative duties.

NOTE

1. For a critical understanding of the effectiveness and appropriateness of student feedback, see Valsan, C. and Sproule, R. (2008), 'The invisible hands behind the student evaluation of teaching: the rise of the new managerial elite in the govern-ance of higher education', *Journal of Economic Issues*, 42(4), pp. 939–58.

72. Teach something that would be useful for you

If you are lucky enough to have the opportunity to teach something slightly out of your comfort zone and beyond your immediate area of expertise and knowledge, it is plausible that you could gain a considerable amount of extra useful knowledge during your teaching preparations. For instance, if you are inquisitive and open-minded enough to understand social science issues from different theoretical and empirical perspectives, then you may be lucky enough to have the opportunity to teach modules such as Contending Perspectives[1] or Research Methods.[2]

Teaching a module like Research Methods can inspire you to collect more appropriate data for your own research and can move you away from relying only on secondary data. Such a module can enable you to showcase your own research to the students and enthuse them even further.

Teaching these critical and reflective modules can enable you to spark the students' analytical minds and inspire them to undertake their own research, perhaps for their research project/dissertation, and answer particular thought-provoking questions.

If you are a theorist, teaching a module like applied marketing, applied business models, applied psychology or applied sociology may enable you to consider actively how you can apply your theory to the real world.

If you are an applied researcher, the opportunity to teach a theoretical module may enable you to reflect on the appropriateness and limitations of connecting the applied nature of research to the breadth of underlying theory, and then question the extent to which an applied result is necessarily exclusive for a particular theory.

Being open to alternative teaching opportunities is sometimes difficult, especially when it forces you to adopt an academic stance that differs from one you are used to. However, sometimes these opportunities pay off in the long term by providing you with further research ideas.

For example, I read the work of Ziliak and McCloskey (2008)[3] and Birks (2015)[4] and became increasingly pessimistic about the accuracy and power of econometric analysis. I was subsequently asked to teach

Econometrics because of the desire for team teaching within a department and there appeared to be no one else in the department who was able to take on this role. This experience spurred me on to co-author a book called *Problems with Econometrics that You Are Rarely Told.*[5] The moral of this story is that frequently you can turn unfortunate circumstances to your advantage, and that includes duties for which you think you are positioned very poorly. Most junctures can be beneficial to you if you have the space and tenacity to turn teaching adversities into positive opportunities.

During professional development reviews, mentors and research leaders should identify gaps in a researcher's teaching portfolio that can be filled to augment their academic knowledge and thereby strengthen the department. Of course, the research leader may have their dominant eye on research, but a broader awareness of the teaching side of duties will be beneficial to the researcher over the long term.

NOTES

1. See, for example, Harvey, J. T. (2020), *Contending Perspectives in Economics: A Guide to Contemporary Schools of Thought*, Edward Elgar Publishing.
2. See, for example, Saunders, M., Thornhill, A. and Lewis, P. (2018), *Research Methods for Business Students*, Pearson.
3. Ziliak, S. T. and McCloskey, D. N. (2008), *The Cult of Statistical Significance*, University of Michigan Press.
4. Birks, S. (2015), *Rethinking Economics: From Analogies to the Real World*, Springer.
5. Webber, D. J. and Thomas, W. (2023), *Problems with Econometrics that You Are Rarely Told.*

73. Recognise the breadth of content in similar modules elsewhere

There are a number of contrasting ways to establish, prepare and teach a module. One standard way is to identify, source and then use a textbook. Students appreciate this pattern, because a textbook is a clear source to which they can refer regularly.

However, once this has been achieved and you have run the module for a couple of semesters, it is worth exploring how the content of such a module differs from comparative modules in competing institutions. Sometimes modules that on the face of it should be similar may instead cover quite disparate topics or be discussed from distinctly different philosophical positions. A rotation of topics (and even potentially philosophical positions) can enhance the interests of the lecturer, preventing the module from becoming stale, reinvigorating the module and increasing student evaluation scores.

The rotation of topics within a module, particularly when that module is close to the research interests of the lecturer, can keep the lecturer on their toes and abreast with up-to-date topics. This alternation of topics will keep the proactive lecturer interested in the subject and heighten their level of expressed enthusiasm within lessons, thereby leading to more enthused students. It will expand the lecturer's understanding of adjacent topics and can encourage the lecturer to consider connections with their own research topic. Actively engaged lecturers will use this new or updated teaching knowledge to their research advantage.

New topics for discussion in modules can be identified through dialogue with colleagues inside and outside a department. A conscientious and trained lecturer will recognise the benefits of regularly rotating topics within modules to freshen up the content, not least to enable new assessment questions. A good source of different topics can often be sourced from supplementary textbooks that approach a topic from a different school of thought.

Another point to consider is the interests of students. I was once asked about 'conscientious consumption' and recognised that, at that time, there was hardly any reference to this topic in relevant textbooks but decided to respond by adapting a seminar so that it included content on the subject (based on information sourced from journal articles) in order to highlight the extent of existing knowledge on the topic. Being responsive to the interests and requests of students keeps the content of the module up to date and ensures that it is of interest and relevant to contemporary students.

Research leaders can contribute here too, but they are unlikely to know the content of individual modules. They can, of course, support the Head of Department in recommending the best practice of regular rotation of topics within modules and by emphasising the benefits of this rotation for research-active staff. Modules that are research-led also benefit from the rotation of topics, and a research leader could suggest to a lecturer that they could include in their module some content from a recent staff seminar.

74. Read around the topic

Some lecturers present information in a way that suggests it is indisputable and undeniable. Presenting anything in a way that is purely objective and utterly correct assumes that the metrics and method of measurement are themselves incontestable. Yes, the number of people classified as being unemployed may be entirely accurate based on the method applied, but research is not about counting, it is about interpreting and improving understanding. So, following this example, it is not how many people who are unemployed that is an interesting issue, but knowing how effective policies are in reducing unemployment, and also why their effectiveness is not the focus of attention.

One of the many beautiful characteristics of the social sciences is that the vast majority of social science issues are available for discussion. This includes the perceived importance of theories, researchers' choices, justification of methods and especially the interpretation of quantitative and qualitative results. Reading around the topic, reinterpreting results from different perspectives, bringing in ideology and values, recognising when we are measuring something that is either unmeasurable with accuracy (such as values) or so trivial that it shouldn't be the focus of measurement enables us to keep our feet on the ground. Focusing on topics that have meaning, understanding the value of interpreting data using different perspectives and redeploying our efforts away from the pedantic can all enhance the usefulness of our teaching and research. Most importantly, we should not be teaching our students what to think, but instead we should be trying to enhance their thinking and reflection skills to help them to arrive at informed decisions.

This focus on real-world and contemporary important issues from different standpoints can enable you to bring insights to your lessons and heighten your students' and your own interests in the content of the module. Make no mistake, in the social sciences we are not teaching our students simply to learn by rote particular methods or to understand something from one monist perspective;[1] we should be teaching our students to understand various perspectives and be agile between theories,[2] to recognise and respect alternative perspectives for what they are and to open their minds to different ways of thinking. It is the understanding of the *why*s that are important, not the creation of clones to maintain our current and potentially deficient way of thinking.

One of the most difficult things to do in the classroom, and also the most undervalued, is teaching content in a controversial and challenging way. It is relatively easy to teach something so that students appreciate the importance of a metric or an order of implementing a technique. A much higher level of teaching skills is required to impel students to question what they already know, to teach them to be critical, to recognise gaps in understanding and to ask them to present a view that opposes their own in a compelling way. These skills require agile and flexible thinking that does not necessarily conform to the established majority.

 Research leaders will be aware of contending perspectives in their own disciplines and will be able to encourage new lecturers, especially those who have received a relatively monist education through topics, to insert different theoretical and ontological perspectives into their modules. This guidance can improve the teaching quality but there will also be spillovers of knowledge into the research-led lecturer's own research.

NOTES

1. Dusek, T. (2008), 'Methodological monism in economics', *Journal of Philosophical Economics*, 1(2), pp. 26–50.
2. See, for example, Harvey, J. T. (2020), *Contending Perspectives in Economics: A Guide to Contemporary Schools of Thought*, Edward Elgar Publishing.

75. Question underlying assumptions

All models and pieces of evidence within the social sciences are subject to some interpretation, not least due to the underlying assumptions of an implicit or explicit model; this needs to be clear to our students. Even when a critical realism approach is chosen as the perspective to investigate a topic, the approach needs to be questioned concerning whether it reveals insightful and useful understanding, and whether greater abstraction would be desirable to illustrate a point. Relaxing underlying assumptions will also push you to understand the depth and breadth of the teaching topic, and this can be very rewarding and enlightening.

Models often create overgeneralisations and are based on limited or misleading theories of causality set within closed systems. A standard assumption is *ceteris paribus*, which means holding all else equal, but of course this assumption never applies in reality because we are living in a dynamically amazing society that is ever changing, and this evolution is the beauty that often we seek to observe and understand. Assuming away uncertain societal evolution leads to the discussion and description of a sterile, hypothetical and unrealistic world. Students will appreciate lectures that highlight illustrations of critical thought, especially when it is over and above the content of a textbook, because it will enhance the value of attending classes.

It is difficult to teach critical thinking skills; one reason for this is that a depth of understanding is required beforehand. But teaching in an uncritical way dumbs down the value of knowledge, trivialises real-world analyses and evaluations, and provides a false sense of security that something can be achieved in an easy manner simply by not recognising the importance of real-world complexities. Some lecturers do not think we should be teaching complex thinking at lower levels of a degree, as it is too difficult for the students (and potentially too challenging for the lecturers!?). Yet the difficulty is not so much about getting students to understand complex matters – they are often much more able than we can ever assume – as it is about identifying how to put that knowledge across in a way that they understand. This is not a challenge for the students; it is a challenge for the engaged lecturer.

It is often the case that we do not fully appreciate the limitations in our underlying assumptions until we realise that our predictions are way off the mark. Most of us are guilty of not realising the importance of key assumptions in our analyses, but some researchers are more open than others to recognising the importance of assumptions.

Research leaders should be at the forefront of recognising and appreciating the importance of underlying theoretical assumptions that underpin a theoretical stance, and should have the ability to unpick the importance of those assumptions in a way that enhances realism and understanding. Research leaders should assist their colleagues by guiding them to implicit assumptions, helping to unravel them and aiding the progression of knowledge.

76. Try to teach in a pluralist way

It is vitally important for lecturers to question knowledge within their lectures and seminars. Many academics cannot conceive that there is value is thinking in any way other than the mainstream. The certainty that some academics have that they know the truth, or that they know the only method to reveal the truth, can be astounding and is contrary to the quest for open thought that universities pride themselves on.

It is easier to focus our lessons on the content of mainstream textbooks and avoid putting yourself in a position to be controversial and contentious. Indeed, today's litigious society even encourages us to resort back to core texts that often phrase things so tightly that they limit wider thought. Yet, the purpose of university education should not be simply to provide information but instead to encourage students to think, compare, contrast and debate to enhance understanding as well as to recognise that most social science knowledge is open to improvement and debate.

There is a diversity of thinking about most social science issues, and recognition of this diversity can lead to research to address those debates and question whether the (apparent) weaker perspectives are underexplored and underappreciated, with social norms swaying us to think about issues that our academic peers recognise as important. Acknowledging a breadth of ideas enables us to emphasise that differences matter and have worth, which can increase tolerance and acceptance of others' ideas.

Teaching in a pluralist way stimulates students to challenge their understanding of mainstream texts, which can lead to deeper understanding of mainstream issues and/or the enthralment in heterodox views. Teaching in a pluralist way is a challenge to yourself and your students, and this can generate a plethora of new ideas and deep and thought-provoking debate that are simply not possible when teaching from a single ontology, ideology or epistemology. There is the view that too much consensus in a discipline can also lead to the stagnation of thought and a movement towards pedantic[1] enquiry,[2] thereby leading to smaller and smaller contributions to knowledge through research activities.

Unfortunately, many core textbooks tend to build on one world view, and if you decide to steer your module towards a more open platform this will make you appear unusual in

the department, especially when you are not surrounded by similarly intellectually open-minded colleagues. Negru (2009) recognises developments in the
philosophy of science, the disarray in economic methodology, the consequent
pleading for tolerance in economics and the wider orthodoxy–heterodoxy
debate as key factors in shaping the nature and direction of the pluralism
debate in economics.[3]

 Often, research within departments can be from a very
similar world view. If this is the case, then nonconformists
may not feel comfortable enough to voice their concerns or
speak up about the limitations of persistently adopting a monist
view. This lack of an open culture that welcomes different
opinions may have disastrous consequences for the progression and the criti-
cality of thought within a department. Research leaders should ensure that all
their colleagues have the support to speak up and voice their alternative views
when they have them.

NOTES

1. "There are two types of people in this world: pedants and everyone else": Petelin,
   R. (2017), 'In defence of grammar pedantry', *The Conversation*, 1 June.
2. Hodgkinson, G. P., Herriot, P. and Anderson, N. (2001), 'Re-aligning the stakeholders in management research: lessons from industrial, work and organisational
   psychology', *British Journal of Management*, 12, pp. s41–s48.
3. Negru, I. (2009), 'Reflections on pluralism in economics', *International Journal
   of Pluralism and Economics Education*, 1(1–2), pp. 7–21.

77. Ensure you teach the *why*s (and not simply the *what*s)

It is very tempting to teach excessive amounts of detail, and perhaps over-complicate lessons. This can make it easier to mark things that are right or wrong in coursework and exams, especially in our litigious society. Unfortunately, learning can only descend into a memorisation exercise and trivialise the importance of thinking, deliberating and philosophising in order to create new thought and new opinion.

 It is my view that we have got ourselves into a bit of a quandary in higher education. There seems to be a need to ensure that we teach things that appear obviously correct – as they are presented in core textbooks or in the top journals – but this is at the cost of thinking and expressing ideas that challenge and further our thinking. Instead, we should be teaching our students to consider, deliberate and critically form ideas that express quality of thought.

Today's powerful Internet search engines enable us to find true and fake facts literally at the touch of a few buttons. This relates to applications of theoretical models without concern for the appropriateness of the source data, the suitability of policy implications for the real world and for the external validity of any findings. Teaching the *what*s without any in-depth thinking about the *why*s inevitably leads to a belief in one way of thinking because of the lack of ability to think laterally and critically, and to question the pseudo-facts in front of us.

 If we want to move the world towards a better place, then we need to ensure that we teach our students in an engaged and critical manner. This is challenging for lecturing and research staff because it requires us to keep abreast of the ever-growing voluminous literature that is published by gatekeepers who have a vested interest in maintaining the status quo.

Comprehension of a wide variety of explanations – where the strengths of an explanation depend on the perspective that you adopt to approach a subject – is inevitably easier if you teach modules encompassing topics that are close to your own research areas. When this is not the case, it is a good idea to adopt a range of core and non-mainstream textbooks and journal articles to fully and properly appreciate the breadth and depth of thinking on the topic.

Adopting this approach can mean that either you have a variety of *why*s that underpin the same *what*, or a variety of *why*s and a variety of *what*s; either is perfectly acceptable if you wish to develop critical and open thinking that shapes graduates for innovative real-world problem-solving and lateral thinking.

 Research leaders can encourage less experienced colleagues to appreciate the breadth of thinking that they may not have received in their own training. Research leaders, too, should encourage their colleagues to come forward to discuss the breadth of ideas in an accessible and mutually beneficial way, perhaps in staff seminars. Research leaders should underscore that wider thinking is expected and welcomed in teaching and in research, not only to enhance the development of students' thinking and problem-solving skills, but also to enhance the likelihood that their students also are able to explore and advocate the strengths and weaknesses of a range of views.

78. Teach in a team with a colleague from whom you can learn something

Team teaching has its difficulties and does not always work, especially when lecturers do not take ownership for their own contributions to a module. However, teaching a module as a team can enable specialisation and debate that can lead to higher-level student outcomes. Teaching a module with a colleague who thinks about a discipline in a different way to yourself can generate a strong need to understand an issue in much greater depth.

For instance, if a sociologist and an economist were to co-teach a module on the connection between mental health and employment, there could be some really lively, contrasting, insightful and inspiring discussion that could awaken the recognition of discipline-specific blind spots and unconscious biases.

 When two academics with open minds but who research from different perspectives collaborate to teach a particular module, it is possible to foster a highly engaging and deliberative module that is full of depth and breadth of thought. Modules with content covering contending perspectives that is presented in a civil, respectful manner can exhibit constructive disagreements and foster humble and considerate interactions by onlooking students. Adoption of such a contestable approach to the construction of thought can usefully benefit both students and staff. Students will recognise and appreciate the breadth of thought, while staff will feel compelled to investigate issues in more depth to enhance the quality of their preparations.

 Team teaching can be a huge challenge, especially if the contrasting content is presented to students in parallel, so an alternative is to undertake such a theoretical adventure following a sequence of perspectives. For instance, I used to lead a module where I presented the core mainstream perspective, and an excellent colleague subsequently presented a heterodox perspective that challenged the mainstream view. This team strategy stimulated me to ensure that the clarity of the underlying assumptions of my material was very explicit (and much more explicit than that which appears in mainstream textbooks), and admittedly it was very hard at times to justify those assumptions.

I learnt a huge amount from my colleague simply because of the need to constructively criticise these ideas in more depth. I would always encourage this type of exercise, but it can only be carried out effectively with highly engaged lecturing staff, and that is always best when the lecturing staff are also researching the topic. The opportunities to learn from colleagues are often constrained to short meetings, water-cooler chats or research seminars, but teaching roles can also be important opportunities for mutual and respectful learning.

 The matching of research interests by research leaders can often result in a stronger teaching team. Research leaders can therefore assist the Head of Department in bringing together constructive research synergies that can reinvigorate modules and lead to exciting student learning opportunities.

79. Understand criticisms of the usual topics

Standard textbooks compete to present core knowledge in an increasingly user-friendly and accessible manner. Although many students probably appreciate this clarity, it is also the case that the knowledge becomes standardised and uncontroversial when, in fact, it is simply the discipline's standard way of communicating one way of understanding a principle.

It is unfortunate, therefore, that many students do not recognise some of the principles of these core textbooks as being up for debate. A good thing to be aware of and use are texts that highlight these controversies and offer a more critical view of seemingly incontestable ideas. They also present ways of integrating material into modules that highlight these controversies. These critical texts are often seen as being supplementary texts, and yet the information that they contain should be core for critical modules with the standard ideas being readily available on the Internet.

Although there are some facts across the social sciences that should be known by undergraduates within their disciplines, we should be moving our graduates towards greater engagement and deeper thinking of contemporarily relevant issues. The ability to nurture greater depth of thought can only be attained if we practise and visibly contend with the literature, and thereby educate by example how to critically engage with the literature.

Embedding controversies behind standard ideas stimulates students and staff to cogitate about a module's content in much more depth than is usually the case. An excellent example of critical thinking about econometrics is provided Birks (2015),[1] and why critical thinking about economics exists has been provided by Harvey (2020).[2]

Birks (2015) recognises and then develops three main types of errors that are encountered when using econometrics: inappropriate *A*ssumptions, inaccurate *B*eta estimates, and inappropriate policy *C*onclusions (otherwise referred to as error types A, B and C). Birks presents the information using many examples that makes it an accessible and engaging graduate-level text.[3]

Teaching alternative and contending perspectives can be a challenge for those lecturers who are not pluralists. But pluralists tend to be those academics that appreciate not only the strengths of ideas but also acknowledge their weaknesses. They tend to be more constructively critical of ideas too in ways that academics who are convinced about their own perspective are not. Before our students become attached to a particular perspective, shouldn't we be teaching them to think about all of the contending perspectives first so that they are not forced to think in – or worse, only be properly aware of – only one perspective?

Research leaders should encourage their colleagues to be aware of contending perspectives. The more academics appreciate the contending perspectives surrounding a particular issue, the more they can criticise their own ideas and build stronger and more convincing arguments. Again, this is better undertaken when modules are research-led, so the research leader should be able to engage with the Head of Department in ways that enhance the teaching and research portfolio of the department.

NOTES

1. Birks, S. (2015), *Rethinking Economics: From Analogies to the Real World*, Springer.
2. Harvey, J. T. (2020), *Contending Perspectives in Economics: A Guide to Contemporary Schools of Thought*, Edward Elgar Publishing.
3. A useful set of critical textbooks is available from http://www.worldeconomicsa ssociation.org/textbook-commentaries/alternative-texts/.

80. Engage the students and they will engage you

Some lecturers, especially highly research-active ones, can distance themselves from the pseudo-mundane matter of teaching undergraduate students and carelessly simplify the teaching process to a one-way knowledge dissemination exercise. Such an approach is suboptimal on all fronts; it does not satisfy student demands, it numbs lecturers and it creates a barrier between the lecturer and the students that stops the two-way transfer of inspiration and knowledge.

 Teaching should be a two-way process, where lecturers inspire and are inspired by students. There are few more exhilarating and rewarding teaching moments than when a lecturer can see that their teaching inspires their students and when the students inspire and surprise the lecturer in equal measures. This occurs when students are heavily engaged, interested and perhaps even enthralled by the content of the lectures. I have bounced my research ideas off students during my classes and have been surprised by how their ideas have been so insightful and grounded. In fact, some inspired students' comments have even led me to research topics in a slightly different way and could have been the inspiration for eventual research papers. When we are not afraid to treat lessons as a two-way conversation and co-creation opportunity, we can create an energising classroom that creates mutual benefits for the students and the lecturer.

 When lecturers encourage greater student engagement (which they should do all of the time) and teach a research-led or research-informed module that is closely linked to their own research interests, so the students' comments can inspire the lecturer to think about their own research in a different way.

Try to engage and inspire your students all of the time; some students seem to be present mainly to be inspired.

I have been very lucky in teaching some excellent students who have questioned understanding in unusual ways, who probed the direction of research and knowledge, who interrogated the ontological and epistemological underpinnings of research and who even revealed gaps in the literature that required (or still require) further research. Teaching is a two-way conversation with two-way benefits.

Lecturers who engage with their students tend to be better in engaging with a conference audience too, and hence research leaders have an interest in ensuring that research-active lecturers maintain an engaging and inspirational teaching approach.

Lecturers hone their teaching style and often unconsciously use that same communication style when they present their research at conferences and within staff seminars. Ensuring that the lecturer uses their presentation skills regularly to inspire students can also ensure that their conference presentation style inspires delegates at conferences.

PART IX

Academic research is related to externally funded work

If you are lucky enough to win an external grant or be approached by an organisation that wishes to use your knowledge, celebrate this achievement. Undertaking externally funded research[1] can be very beneficial for your career trajectory, but be careful not to fall into a few traps and become known as a consultant without any critical academic thought, and do ensure that you do not lose sight of the fact that you are an academic rather than a consultant. Some funders simply want a prestigious academic stamp on a document rather than your insight.

NOTE

1. Throughout this text, I refer to externally funded research as any research that an organisation is paying you to do. This excludes research council grants, such as the AHRC, ESRC and EPSRC. Research Councils tend to fund research that you propose, rather than ask you to research something on their behalf.

81. Recognise that externally funded work takes time away from academic research

You will need to ensure that you achieve on a variety of fronts as you progress further in your career. These fronts include good-quality teaching, publications in world-leading journals, effective contributions to the running of your department/faculty/university and income generation. Progress and achieve a good level of quality on each front in that order. Trying to progress on too many fronts at once can take time away from your academic research, which can have a detrimental impact on your research career.

 Each of these four areas of expertise takes time to develop, improve and master. By mastering the first three before you master the fourth, you will ensure that you do not encounter time- and energy-draining issues that reduce your ability to be proficient in the first three areas. You will not want to let down those external organisations that have decided to financially support your research, nor damage your reputation before it is made.

Networking and attending externally funded project inception meetings, presentations and other forms of dissemination all take a lot of time. Recognition of the full amount of time it takes to undertake externally funded activities might put pure academic researchers off venturing down the external funding route.

 Focus on achieving in teaching, publications, contributions to the department and income generation, in that order. Do not try to generate income until you have achieved in the other areas first, as it will take time and effort away from other activities that you will be judged on before you are judged on income generation. For instance, if you generate external income but cannot publish, you may become known as a consultant rather than as an academic.

Although income generation is undoubtedly an important skill to be documented on your CV, publications in world-leading journals are more highly regarded by academic department recruitment panels. It is advisable, therefore, that once you have a record of accomplishment in income generation, to select carefully which funder you will work for, which contracts you will field out to colleagues and which contracts you will not apply for or consider turning down. The benefit of the extra income stated on your CV may not be worth the loss of high-quality journal output.

 Research leaders are often the people approached to undertake externally funded work. They are also the individuals with the least amount of time to spare and should prioritise providing help and support to their colleagues to build and strengthen the department and help their colleagues achieve their potentials.

Research leaders can strengthen the skills within their department by asking less experienced colleagues to join them on an externally funded research project. A trusted, integrated and supported team is one that will achieve, and a research leader will look stronger under these circumstances than a research leader that is performing in isolation.

82. Is it the right time in your career to undertake the work?

Externally funded activities nearly always take a significantly longer amount of time than you expect. Given that the amount of time you devote to teaching and administration duties are relatively fixed, undertaking externally funded activities will eat into time that you could devote to academic research activities. You need to consider very seriously whether you have time to undertake externally funded activities and what the effect will be on your academic research trajectory.

Clearly, promotion opportunities are more frequent if you have raised external funding, but your academic standing and credibility only come with contributions to knowledge and not whether you write a report for organisation X.

Identify the priorities for you at this stage in your career, essentially deciding which of the following areas of your portfolio you should achieve next: increasing your peer-reviewed journal articles, improving teaching effectiveness and efficiency, extending external funding streams or enhancing peer esteem. Some opportunities will allow you to achieve in more than one of these areas at a time, while others will be clear-cut substitutes for your precious time.

Gain advice from respected academics external to your university, who know you well, and ask them what they would do if they were at your stage in your career. Reflect on their advice, decide whether you should follow it and make sure that you are setting your sights high enough so that you achieve your ambitions.

The greater danger for most of us lies not in setting our aim too high and falling too short, but in setting our aim too low and achieving our mark. (Michelangelo)

Regularly reflect on your research ambitions and whether the path that you are following will reward you in the ways that you want most. Externally funded work can open doors for you; it can provide you with greater freedom and appease your line manager and it can open doors to data that you require but are unable to find elsewhere.

However, undertaking externally funded work at the wrong time can ramp up pressures on you when you should be marking, writing lectures, attending important conferences or taking a well-needed break.

Often it is better to work with excellent and trusted collaborators who you can rely on to take the strain if you do not have the time. Your trusted collaborators will take up the slack when you are unable to, and vice versa. Teamwork often pays off when unexpected events come your way but when external funders still want your work by a strict deadline.

 Here, research leaders can be important conduits and linchpins in several important ways. They can identify opportunities for externally funded research for their colleagues. They can integrate their colleagues into externally funded teams to share the workload and provide experience to colleagues. They can be the 'professor' label on an externally funded document (which is often needed to gain that air of superiority). They can present the work in large public meetings, which can be daunting for less experienced staff.

It is of prime importance that the research leader fully acknowledges the roles and contributions of colleagues that have contributed to the project. This ensures that their colleagues feel valued, appreciated and recognised, which strengthens the department through teamwork.

83. Constrain funded activities to those that could result in an academic publication

It is very important to realise that although academics should provide assistance and guidance to government and the wider social world, we are not judged strongly enough by our knowledge exchange contributions. Instead, research assessment exercises and peer effects continue to ensure that journal publications are the main indicator of our position within academe. Given this, it is vital to consider whether any externally funded work would lead to a quality journal article.

 It is relevant to understand that if you conduct externally funded work that does not lead to a quality journal article, you are simply doing work that a consultant could do. You have not generated new academically relevant publishable knowledge. Consultants are not there to improve academic knowledge; they are there to provide expert advice. Nevertheless, at various points in your career, it may still be the right decision to take on such work.

 The best and most valuable externally funded work that an academic can do will have benefits to both the funder and to academia. Identify the gap in academic knowledge that you could close by fulfilling the externally funded contract and kill two birds with one stone by completing the contract and ensuring that part of that work will lead to a journal output. Ensure that your externally funded contract includes the freedom to publish connected research output in an academic journal.

Recognise that this externally funded work should have strong synergies with academic research and that they should not be substitutes. Make sure that the externally funded work is as complementary as possible to your own academic research interests and that you are not simply following the money.

 Research leaders should support less experienced researchers in their attempts to undertake externally funded work, as it is valuable to their colleague's career and to the department profile. Externally funded research opportunities can make a change to society and should be seen in a very positive light.

However, research leaders should shield their colleagues from undue pressures from universities to raise money. Although raising external funds is undoubtedly an important activity, an academic's career can be stunted if they focus their intellectual efforts simply on fundraising rather than on making important contributions to the academic literature.

84. Work with others on externally funded projects

Many of us will be able to construct a sampling frame, collect data and write up those pieces of research autonomously, but other parts of the externally funded research project, such as the write up of the (non-academic!) report and the (non-academic!) discussion, (non-academic!) presentation and (non-academic!) test phase can be completely alien to most academics.

A different set of skills is required to be successful in fulfilling an externally funded consultancy project. Different people bring diverse skills to an externally funded research team, so it is better to undertake these activities as a team of academics who contribute different skills.

 Externally funded projects require a range of skills that (usually) one academic does not possess. Some academics are excellent at writing grant applications, some are superior at communicating effectively with stakeholders, while others are excellent at undertaking the analysis. As there will be particular externally funded activities that your colleagues will be better at than you are (in relative terms at least), and as it may take you a lot of time and effort to improve your own skills and fulfil all of the roles yourself, it is much better and much more enjoyable to share the workload. This is also an important opportunity for experienced researchers to introduce less experienced academic researchers to the trials and tribulations of externally funded research contracts.

Your colleagues may identify gaps, fill gaps and conduct sensitivity tests that you did not even think of. They may simply lighten the load for you, if not in the short run (when they may need training up), then in the long run. Sharing the workload can enable you to allocate more time to your own academic research agenda.

 The long-term benefits of sharing externally funded work are high, especially if you form a specialist and complementary team that works well together. Once you have invested time in completing your first collaborative project, the second and subsequent ones should be easier because you know your team's strengths, although there will of course be contract-specific challenges that keep you engaged and interested.

My suggestion, therefore, is that you start or integrate yourself into an effective and flexible team as early as you can, where each individual has their own distinct role. Trust in colleagues is key here: trust that they will complete tasks with time to spare so that each colleague can inspect the work, trust that they will do their best and trust that they will not let the rest of the team down. Pick your team wisely to save time and stress later.

 Research leaders will have expertise in several areas but, for the good of the department, they should invite their colleagues to work with them on externally funded projects. By collaborating on activities, research leaders can make sure that they are not stretching themselves too thin and are giving colleagues new opportunities and new experiences to work on externally funded projects.

Research leaders should have three main roles: first, they should be the person securing the funding and having the highly credible reputation; second, they should be excellent mentors who motivate their colleagues to do their best; and third, they need to provide effective guidance to their colleagues to enhance the effectiveness of the externally funded research experience to increase the strength of the department in the long run.

85. Identify what a contractor wants

As academics, our primary aim is to contribute to knowledge. We enjoy opportunities to explore and to discover something new. Some external funders do want you to discover new knowledge within their spheres of influence and interest, but at other times they simply want you to reveal evidence that is consistent with their aims.

Some funders have some spare cash that they need to spend by the end of a financial year but do not know fully what they want from you; they start with a rough idea, then you tell them the answer to that rough idea and then they demand more. Others have their own agenda and do not want you to use your investigative skills; they simply want you to provide evidence that supports their political, economic, commercial and/or social aims.

 For a novice, being asked to provide some externally funded work appears to be a big compliment, with the funder initially being very flattering about how interesting and useful your research has been to date.

However, be aware that some funders endeavour to push you to fulfil additional requirements. As you will want to ensure that they are pleased with your work, you may agree do a little bit more than originally agreed. Further down the line they may ask for some further changes and a bit more here and there, all of which they will phrase as though they were part of the original agreement.

In my experience, this is especially the case when you reveal results that are not consistent with what they expect/want. You may then have slight doubts about sample size, or the potential for bias in the sample, and you may then proceed to carry out more work to fulfil the contract. You need to accept that they might never be satisfied with your work unless your results comply fully with their perspective. This will drain you of energy and make you wish that you had never started the work. Sometimes it is best to agree to cut your losses, simply to regain your sense of purpose.

To ensure that this does not happen, do not sign the form confirming that you will do the work until you know exactly what they are looking for, that you agree with them that this research is investigative and may not generate the results that they desire, and that you all know exactly the work to be performed.

Always, and without fail, make sure that your contract has a clear exit point, and that this relates to a clear fulfilment of stated aims. Reflect on all aspects of the work before you undertake the work – it could save you a huge amount of time and energy. Never sign a contract that has no clear exit point. Other than work for research councils, always be sceptical about whether the work is truly and genuinely exploratory, or whether there is some hidden motive.

Ensure that every contract has a clear cut-off point after which you will not provide further work, and then stick to it. If the funder wants you to extend the work, that will require a new contract with a new exit point.

Research leaders should be aware that external funders tend to want more than they initially ask for. An optimist would suggest that these are simply justifiable sensitivity tests or similar, whereas a realist would suggest that they are simply trying to gain an increase in value for money.

Research leaders need to be on hand to use their experience to advise on the wording of contracts (what it means from the discipline's perspective rather than the university's lawyers' perspective) and the work needed to fulfil the duties. They should be available to provide advice and guidance on all externally funded work, because the junior academic (and many senior ones!) may feel under pressure to provide more than they bargained for; after all, many social scientists want to give back to society. Initial externally funded experiences can shape future engagements and will affect an academic's ability to raise future external funds.

86. Facts, explanations and political rhetoric

Many external research funding organisations will want you to identify *what* is happening rather than *why* that something is happening, and then ask you to comment on whether a particular policy lever could be appropriate.

 In essence, many of them will be asking you to confirm their suspicions and to corroborate their view that a particular action is necessary. They may steer you towards looking at a specific case or policy implementation rather than a competing example or policy alternative. Often there will be political issues that underlie these requests, which you may not be aware of.

 If you are a number cruncher who uses secondary data, typically with periodic updates, then you may be in a very good position to produce updates of documents to guide their policy initiatives. However, if you tend to collect detailed primary qualitative data or if you wish to understand the underlying breadth of possibilities and being closer to having full knowledge, you may not fully appreciate the boundedness of some externally funded research experiences.

Being aware of possible underlying political issues or potential policy implementations before you start is vital. You may be able to produce a piece of empirical work that is based on a particular ontology and epistemology and the result follows naturally from a certain set of underlying assumptions. You may be drawn into producing something that, in hindsight, you may feel uneasy with, even if the results are clear to you, simply because they are overextending the interpretation of your results. You may be unaware that your results are being reinterpreted in a particular way to claim support for something that you do not stand for, or that you find distasteful.

Further, you may produce results and claims that do not concur with their expectations, and this could lead them to ask a critical reviewer to undermine your argument and claims. You may then be drawn into an ideological debate that has profile, and this is unlikely to be what you signed up for!

Less experienced staff may need the support of their research leaders on some pieces of externally funded work, especially when the results prove to be controversial to the funder. Research leaders need to have the confidence and standing to be able to step in and assist their colleagues while also being able to smooth the waters and not lose future contracts.

Some issues can be a political hot potato, and Vice Chancellors may need to step in to make decisions to keep high profile and powerful external funders on their side. Confidential agreements to ensure that contentious results are not disclosed outside of the externally funded research team and the funders are not unheard of.

87. Prepare to present information to non-academics

Academics are trained to communicate academic ideas to other academics (i.e. university staff) or to academics in training (i.e. students). Our standard training is not geared towards the communication of academic ideas to non-academics; sometimes it feels that academics and policymakers are using different languages. To enhance the effectiveness of your communication of ideas to non-academics, you must enrol in effective training to re-engineer your expectations and vocabulary.

 Academics tend to be interested in detail that we can deliberate, reflect on and debate, and some of these technicalities may be described by others as being 'purely academic' or even 'pedantic'. Non-academics and many policymakers, however, are mostly interested in the substantive nature of information and what it can mean for them and their jurisdiction.

The potential gulf in interests between academics and non-academics should influence the way that you communicate your ideas and concerns to non-academics. For instance, some academics may not be able to understand why some policymakers may not appreciate something that they find very interesting and potentially useful to the policymaker, while the policymaker may become frustrated by an overly precise result which an academic may not wish to extrapolate out of sample.

 Most academics will find this type of communication training useful. Poor communication skills can cost follow-on funding opportunities because of the frustration that is inherent in the poor communication of ideas. Many universities train academics to communicate with the media, and often these skills come in useful when communicating with external funders too.

Of course, external funders typically want more specific engagement about a topic than the media require. Having the ability to communicate to different audiences is challenging, often requires training to be effective and typically requires regular practice. When academics communicate effectively with non-specialists, they can become household names, such as Professor

Alice Roberts, Professor Brian Cox, Dr Maggie Aderin-Pocock and Dr Lucy
Worsley.

 Learning how to communicate effectively with external funders seems to come with practice and the development of mutual respect. Some universities do fund such training opportunities, although these skills often improve with practice and through the emulation of more senior colleagues. Research leaders should recommend such training to relevant staff and invite colleagues to work on externally funded work with them.

88. Build links with an organisation that you wish to help

Network with organisations that you wish to support, perhaps because they stand for something that you believe in, or have values similar to your own. Many value-driven organisations will be pleased that an academic wishes to support them, and this can also raise your peer esteem as well as opportunities for external funding. You are most likely to be inquisitive and highly engaged when your values align strongly with the values held by the funder.

 Your preferred funders should be those that recognise and respect your contributions to knowledge and are able to fund your time to think about their problem or issue. Respect is often mutual, so their respect for your ideas may be because you respect their efforts and what they stand for; potential examples could include Greenpeace or the World Wide Fund for Nature.

Funded research that does not lead to journal publication may be of questionable value for your personal CV, but it can provide you with immense pride that you have helped to save an environment, contributed to changing a policy for the better or opened doors for other highly competent people to make a positive change to society. This pride can be compounded by opportunities to undertake research with organisations in areas that you feel personally are vital for the positive progression of society, and in an area that you wish to have impact.

 Once you are established as a recognised academic, you will have opportunities to make a beneficial difference to society. Make time to reflect on what impact you would like to make and with/for whom, and then ensure that you build mutually respectful and positive relationships with those organisations so that you can benefit them and, hopefully, they can benefit you. These positive reciprocating ties take time to build.

One benefit of a research assessment exercise that recognises impact is that you do not have to receive external funds to make a difference. Sometimes organisations allow you to have privileged access to their company or individual members, recommend that their contacts engage with you and then enable your research to have a mutually beneficial impact. Via the intricacies of research assessment exercises, unfunded research for an organisation that leads to a high-quality impact case study can be more financially valuable to a university than a series of small externally funded reports because government funds are subsequently allocated based on the quality of the impact. Hence, it is your links to the organisation that may matter most, rather than simply the immediate generation of income for your institution.

 Research leaders are often more successful at bringing in funds for their department than other members of staff. But if research leaders focus most of their efforts on generating funds, they should be aware that their colleagues may consider it to be of a lower priority because of their lack of contributions to the academic literature.

Instead, when research leaders engage with respectable and reputable organisations that are clearly worthy of academic help and then encourage, support and collaborate with colleagues in their department, the benefits and kudos are spread across the department. Ensuring that the organisation's values align with an academic's can generate even more respect for the researching academic.

89. Why would funders contact you specifically?

In the same way that academics should have a focus and be known for that focus within particular groups of academic colleagues, you should also be known to policymakers for producing particular types of reports. Policymakers share policy documents with policymakers from other jurisdictions, and hence policymakers in other jurisdictions may contact you to request a similar piece of research for them. If you can sustain sufficient interest in an area, then this could be a fruitful conveyor belt of externally funded income that you could draw on repeatedly over time.

 When you produce externally funded work of which you are proud, and the knowledge embedded in that report shines through to the external funders, then you will become known to a wide range of stakeholders. To strengthen that name and to ensure longevity, you will need to evolve and augment your offering so that you can continually offer those funders something new.

Sometimes you will need to demand-manage, by emphasising why that new knowledge is vital for them and value for money, but if you have already given them something that they found valuable, you have that all important record of accomplishment. Revising the content of your offering gives the impression to the recipient that you are at the forefront of knowledge.

Ensure that you are not only distinct and up to date, but also visible through a process of effective communication. Ensuring visibility of externally funded work, sometimes through word of mouth and sometimes through documents on your website, can also put you clearly in the market to provide something important. If you highlight that your research outputs are good enough for the market leader or a prestigious funder, it may also be good enough for the next best external funder.

 You should establish your 'brand' as early as you can, so that funders know about your offering, and the more visible that offering is, the more work will come your way. An important way to do this is to actively engage with existing debate and show in those debates that you have something extra to say. Change the dialogue so that the discussion swings around to what you are good at and to the contributions that you are able to provide. Be clear that it has immense value and that the benefits of your research reports outweigh their costs. Establishing that you are influential in the area is key, and your funders will want the most up-to-date knowledge.

One of my very first contributions to external fund-raising research activities was through a senior colleague who wanted to share the burden. I did not want to step on colleagues' toes but did want to pull my own weight in the team. Communication is key in these circumstances, and good communication saves time later. Steadily, through one contract after another, we built a team in which we had mutual trust to complete our own specialist contributions to the end report on time. Collectively we produced reports that built on our prior work and we established a reputation of togetherness and reliability.

90. Can you afford not to undertake externally funded research?

Some academics think that they are above the need to engage in externally funded research. However, social science research should aim to shape real-world policy, contribute to practical and relevant knowledge and help move society forward.

If you are an excellent teacher, publishing in world-leading journals and making effective contributions to the life and administration of your department, your next step should be to contribute to externally funded research and make a significant difference to society. Active researchers cannot afford *not* to do externally funded research if there are opportunities relevant to their research area, as externally funded work can enable your academic research to be implemented in the real world.

 Your understanding, motivating theory, epistemological stance and philosophical perspective can influence policymakers and consultants if it is put to them in a convincing manner. The satisfaction of knowing that you have changed policy and benefited society can be immense. Note that it can also be addictive, and once you start making change for the better, you may become driven to make more change to the benefit of more people.

 In my experience, and contrary to popular opinion, the obstacle that stops academics from engaging with consultants and policymakers is not that they cannot see the relevance and benefits of doing so. When academics recognise and are offered the opportunity to engage with consultants and policymakers, many are open to the chance, conditional upon those opportunities building on, and being strictly complementary to, their own academic research.

There are times in the academic year that are better than others for externally funded research activities. Big research projects are better undertaken out of teaching terms and should not be a substitute for annual leave and seasonal festivals, such as Christmas. However, consultants and policymakers do not work to the same timescales as academics. This can mean that externally funded work needs to be shoehorned into an academic's schedule.

Of course, research leaders should undertake their own relevant externally funded research. But research leaders should also ensure that their colleagues also do the same when relevant but do not burn themselves out. Research leaders who recognise that externally funded work will increasingly be part of a colleague's portfolio of work activities must make the case that their administrative and teaching loads are limited in order to enhance the academic's capacity to fulfil those externally funded work requirements. Research leaders will recognise the difficulties of completing these time-consuming and time-sensitive externally funded activities within normal working hours, and therefore must endeavour to use their position to safeguard the well-being of their colleagues.

PART X

Impact

Impact is all about making a substantive contribution to part or all of society. If your research is good enough, you should be making a beneficial impact on society. If your research is not substantive enough to make that contribution, perhaps you need to ask a bigger or more useful question.

> Don't let your learning lead to knowledge. Let your learning lead to action. (John Rohn)

91. Connect to the real world

Let's face it, sometimes academics work on projects that seem important to us but are actually trivial and practicably irrelevant to Joe Public. Although there is clear space for lateral and imaginative thinking that could have important and substantive contributions to knowledge, and this should still be actively encouraged because it is unknown what we will discover by doing so, we also need to ensure that we connect successfully to the real world.

Connecting to the real world allows us to disseminate our knowledge and discoveries to the rest of society in the form of public talks, knowledge exchange, policy advice and media coverage. Non-academics' questions can inspire us to think about new points and new avenues for research, and often we forget how insightful and relevant Joe Public's questions and points can be.

 Connecting our research to the real world is possible using a wide range of channels. The previous tip emphasises the benefits of connecting to stakeholders and policymakers, but connecting to society and the general public, and creating any beneficial behavioural change, can be achieved through public talks, open debates, the facilitating or chairing of open meetings or simply going out to meet companies, organisations or community groups. Broadening our academic horizons by connecting to the real world can improve our awareness of differences in perspectives, and this enhancement of our own awareness of real-world issues can feed back not only as examples into our teaching but also inform and shape the directions of our research.

When we connect to the real world through council meetings, meetings with chambers of commerce, meetings with local community members, open meetings discussing local pertinent issues and rallies of politically motivated speakers, we come to realise the depth of understanding of key issues that the public already has of a moot point. We can also gain an appreciation of the depth of feeling or extent of their (and our) misunderstanding of an issue. We can correct our own misunderstandings about the perceived importance of particular issues and change the focus of our research so that we either redirect our research to something that now appears to be more relevant to the current day or strengthen our case that an improvement in the dissemination of knowledge, rather than fake news, is warranted.

By sitting in our offices, we miss these knowledge dissemination opportunities and instead are in danger of building theoretical models that have extremely limited relevance to the real world.

Connecting to the real world enables us to generate impact. Of course, impact is not simply the engagement with these non-academic groups, as impact is the change that occurs as a result of your engagement with these groups. Engagement is necessary but not sufficient to create change, so impact does not occur without engagement. There can be a time lag between engagement and impact, and impact is by no means guaranteed to occur immediately after engagement, if at all.

Sometimes change happens when we least expect it. Measuring impact is problematic. Imagine putting a Bunsen burner under a container without the knowledge that the Bunsen burner will heat the liquid in the container; if this is the case then we would not use a thermometer to measure the change. Similarly, if you are unable to guess ex ante the impact of your knowledge exchange with the real world, you will not necessarily measure the change of the parameter before and after your engagement. Gauging impact is an important but challenging activity.

Research leaders need to be able to help colleagues second-guess the possible effects of engagement with the real world. They should be advising their colleagues what to look out for and how to measure any change. This takes skill, knowledge and experience, and is often invaluable for the creation of an impact case for research assessment exercises.

92. External engagement and knowledge exchange

If you wish to use your research to create a beneficial change to society, you will need to engage with stakeholders and policymakers. Exchanging knowledge with these groups facilitates the transfer of knowledge that can move society forward. This requires you to engage with policymakers and exchange your knowledge with them, to encourage them to shape and improve policies and to make a beneficial difference to people's lives. It also enables you to support your communities. The Economic and Social Research Council (ESRC) defined knowledge exchanges as a two-way exchange of ideas, research evidence, experiences and skills between researchers and research users.

 Exchanging ideas can create benefits for both the academic and the users of the academic's knowledge. As academics, we tend to value our knowledge and we recognise that stakeholders and policymakers could use our knowledge when setting or nudging their own agenda in the right direction. However, we do not necessarily prioritise disseminating that knowledge outside of academia.

Less experienced academics sometimes do not appreciate that these knowledge exchanges provide huge personal benefits. By imparting our ideas to the engaged and listening ears of stakeholders and policymakers, we are able to test that knowledge and identify whether this is new or old knowledge, whether the contribution is really substantive or purely academic, whether the knowledge is respected and acceptable, and/or whether we are missing something significant in our own analyses and understanding of the world. Policymakers and stakeholders can inform the academic about information that they are aware of, perhaps filling a blind spot in the academic's knowledge. In contrast, a policymaker or stakeholder may benefit from receiving that academic knowledge, including the nuances, and receiving the knowledge drawn perhaps from meta-analysis studies from across the world. Policymakers and stakeholders are also exceptionally good at identifying new problems for academics to cogitate on, and in my experience these tend to be context-specific examples about when policy might not have the effect that we think it should, or about practical barriers to the application of other proposed policy recommendations.

Academics should prioritise the type of knowledge exchange that would create the most beneficial impact on society. Being on the knowledge exchange circuit empowers you to identify who you can interact with most effectively while increasing your knowledge of the most efficient channels for knowledge exchange. Frequent interaction with stakeholders and policymakers creates opportunities for mutually beneficial activities, such as the distribution and analysis of surveys of members to enhance understanding, access to participants to enhance the sample size of different data collection projects, occasions to engage with wider society and opportunities for stakeholders and policymakers to provide down-to-earth lectures on your teaching modules.

 Research leaders should be highly engaged with policymakers. They should already be exchanging knowledge and deepening their engagement with non-academics for the betterment of society. One of the roles of research leaders is to open these doors to their colleagues in order to enhance further the engagement of members of the department with stakeholders and policymakers.

93. Research practical and useful issues

There is clearly a place for academic, theoretical, highbrow research; this is undeniable. However, there is arguably greater urgency for research that nudges policies forward and that have a high level of relevance to contemporary society and for the reduction of society's woes.

 Your ability to make some real-world impact is dependent on your ability to undertake practical and relevant research. It is very difficult to make a socially beneficial impact if you stay in your ivory tower, disconnected from society. We should all make a space in our research for practical research that has immediate relevance to society, and there are so many aspects that we can improve upon.

 Another important aspect to remember is that many beneficial policy recommendations are only implemented if they are supported by power and money. Undertaking practical and relevant research can mean that your analyses and subsequent policy recommendations will be actively undermined by people who perceive that those policies do not benefit them directly, and so would rather prioritise other policies.

However, if your research is vitally important to large swathes of society, such as the homeless, those in poverty, those without permanent shelter or those who are socially excluded, then you need to speak up, be heard and have the confidence that what you are doing is right for society. Whenever you think that you have something good to say, and can make a beneficial change, then have courage and be brave.

 Research leaders may need to be on hand to provide support to their colleagues and encourage them to research real-world issues. They may also need to support those colleagues who are undermined by people in power and with money who have the ability, drive and resources to undermine quality academic research. The maintenance of a supportive and engaged academic culture can enable us to be brave and strive to make a beneficial difference.

94. Be conscious of what your research could be used for

Imagine that you conduct and complete your research in goodwill, you undertake the work with the upmost integrity and responsibility and you provide a report that you think is clear and concise. You recognise that your work is conditional on the quality of the data; it will typically be a within sample analysis and be context specific. You interpret the results in this way and urge caution to the organisation in the wider interpretation of those results.

Unfortunately, it is not unusual for external funding organisations to then interpret your results out of context. It is even possible that they extend the interpretation of your information so that the knowledge is misconstrued and used to support a policy that you are completely against ethically and morally. Be careful and be conscious: your research may be used to justify something that you may be very uneasy about!

 Some organisations want a report written by a credible academic that they can use to back up their own policy decisions. However, they may not tell you what that policy decision is or what your report is going to be used for. Their policy decision may be consistent with the results that you provide, but your results may not necessarily point to that policy decision and instead your work could point to a range of other possible policy recommendations, including some that are morally preferable.

Keep an eye on the news and other social media and try to imagine how your report could be used. Do insert into those documents statements that make clear what your report does *and* does not mean, and make sure that these statements clarify that you are not supporting a particular policy recommendation that you do not want to be associated with.

 It is possible to become a pawn in a funding organisation's game, and you become a puppet that enables them to meet their agenda and strengthen their claims. The alignment of your own values with theirs needs to be clear, and anything else can create anxiety and stress, and lead you to wonder what your peers would think of you if they perceived that you supported, for example, a particular socially distasteful policy.

As we progress in our work, we become increasingly cognisant of institutional layers, of the role of power in accomplishing a strategy and the importance of reputation. Some academics simply want to create an income stream for their academic institution in order to increase the chance that they achieve a promotion; others prioritise only working on those research areas that are associated with clear improvements in policy and direction for society. Most academics lie (partly unconsciously) somewhere between these two extremes.

Although academic structural pressures exist that push us into fulfilling income-generating contracts, we do need to ensure that we are happy with the consequences of our actions, including those that we participated in inadvertently. Greater awareness of factors that we would normally be oblivious to is therefore key, and this can come about through discussion with a variety of potentially interested and often contending parties.

 Keeping colleagues up to date with changes in reputations of funding organisations can be key to the successful completion of contracts and to the maintenance of the reputation of a department. Recognition of negative news stories, unfavourable policies, instances of poor reputation and complications that have adverse effects for proportions of society are all worthy of cogitation and reflection about whether you, personally and professionally, want to be associated with that organisation.

Research leaders need to ensure that their colleagues have sufficient knowledge and feel able to react to information about reputations, not least because it reflects on the department and the university. It is important that we stand for something that is morally valuable, and this can mean saying no to external funding opportunities that align with something that we do not agree with, even if it means that a promotion opportunity will be missed this time around. It is more important to safeguard your reputation and feel morally comfortable with the work that you are doing and what it might be used for.

95. Volunteer without payments/pay-offs

Sometimes organisations will not have the financial ability to support your research or to pay you to conduct research for them. If you have a strong ethical and moral drive to contribute to their aims and objectives, you should consider using your time, energy and expertise to support their vision anyway.

Even if you are not paid by the organisation to do some work, you could gain a lot of satisfaction from doing the work for an organisation that you think is making an important contribution to society and whose values align with your own. You could gain subsequent publications out of your work, and you could even generate an impact case study for a research assessment exercise.

Often pro bono work leads to an enhancement of the researcher's reputation because people recognise that the work is carried out in kind and that the researcher recognises and values things other than financial gain. It can take a lot of time to undertake this type of voluntary work, but the satisfaction that you receive once the work is completed can be second to none.

Do not do too much of this voluntary work for non-paying organisations, however, as it may spread the word that you will do work for free. Organisations may ask you to do work for them for free when in fact they do have money available to pay for your services. If you focus all of your efforts on providing support, time and your expertise to create a noble and worthy contribution, you will have less time to devote to other areas that lead to promotion.

Promotions, especially to full professor, can benefit the cause for two reasons: first, you will have a higher profile and this means that people will listen to your opinions more, which can come in handy when you are trying to support a cause. Second, promotion often provides you with more flexible time (e.g. away from teaching) which can again enable you to make a more concrete and uninterrupted contribution to helping those causes you believe in and can help with.

When I was a junior staff member, I knew a research leader who did some work for a global non-governmental environmental organisation. I was really pleased that the research leader was providing their expertise to that organisation because it was clear that they thought there was a strong similarity between their own values and the values of that organisation. This example informed me from a relatively early career stage that we can strive to do good in society and use our academic knowledge proactively. This was an excellent example to show a junior member of staff, but I was surprised how few people knew about this good work, because it really boosted my appreciation of that research leader.

96. Prove that you have instigated a change in others' behaviour

Research assessment exercises often require you to prove that you have made a difference to a part of society in the form of an impact case study. Being able to prove that you have made a substantive effect on policymakers or on other aspects of society can be a sizeable challenge, not least because you need to measure the situation before *and* after in order to generate measurable evidence. Best practice is to ensure that you have a set of baseline indicators prior to any intervention.

 When you make an important, measurable impact, and when other people can see the scale of your impact, others may also want you to make a measurable and positive impact on their organisation too. The stronger the impact, the more that they will be willing to pay you to affect that impact.

Stronger reputations of impact, and greater knowledge of how to create that impact, can then be transferred to organisations that you would really like to help make a change for the better. Without proof of impact, people will perceive that you do not have much influence, and therefore they will prioritise making contact and engaging with other academics. As you begin to establish a track record, more opportunities will flow your way.

 Impact is often only measurable by association, and therefore it can be questionable. Perhaps the organisation was going to make that change anyway, but just needed you to provide evidence that doing so was the right thing to do. Sometimes you expect to make a contribution in one area, but the effect is found in another unexpected area, and therefore measurable evidence is not possible because you didn't establish a baseline measure in that area.

The important issue is that you are able to measure something that is due to your own work and contribution. This can mean spending a lot of time measuring the initial situation in order to create a baseline, and this effort can seem tedious if it is in an area in which you are unlikely to have an effect. Nevertheless, time spent constructing a data baseline can enable you to prove impact and can save an inordinate amount of time later trying to prove the impact your research has had retrospectively.

Research leaders can use their experience to help and guide their colleagues on which baseline areas to look at to gauge impact. Research leaders should be able to contribute to the process of lateral thinking in order to suggest areas that less experienced researchers may not have thought about when considering how to measure impact. Similarly, it is often the case that less experienced researchers are able to think of areas to measure impact that experienced researchers may not have thought about. Thus, open, critical and supportive interaction between colleagues across the seniority rank is important when holding brainstorming sessions, where the aim is to identify what to look for and how to measure impact.

97. Team up with non-academics/ policymakers

Many academics purposefully or unintentionally live, at least to some extent, disconnected from the real world. Sometimes we are able to distance ourselves from reality and focus on our abstract theoretical models. Although academics may be relatively good at knowing theory, we may often be relatively poor at fully appreciating contextual factors.

Some of the best people to ask about contextual factors are local policymakers, councillors, chambers of commerce, citizen advice bureaus, taxi drivers, general people in the street, etc. The sorts of people you choose to team up with will depend on the topic that you are investigating. Teaming up with groups of non-academics can encourage you to reflect on different issues and enable you to identify academically interesting nuances that may disconnect theoretical expectations from practice; these opportunities can also inspire you to write up these nuances and reflections for disseminations to others.

 We can only create impact, enhance understandings and contribute to society if we fully understand a situation. However, there are different views on the order of priority and the contributory effects of various issues. To gauge an understanding of this broad range of real or imaginary issues, the best thing to do is to go out and ask people, discuss the issues with those people who are most affected by an issue and talk to people who are most responsible for any change in policy.

The difficult thing here, however, is making sure that you engage with the right people at the right time, and that those people are representative of that particular group. For instance, the best way to understand the reasons why people voted for and against Brexit is to go out and ask them. Some of those arguments you may not understand or agree with, but your role is to understand their perspective on the issue, irrespective of whether it is real or imagined.

The underlying reasons for your engagement with non-academics and policymakers are therefore to increase your own understanding and to contribute your knowledge to relevant policymakers to stimulate, document, guide or recommend a beneficial change to society. Even if you are unsuccessful in supporting change, it is entirely possible that putting those challenges on paper for other people to read can increase the depth of debate and understanding, and thereby lay a foundation for future changes for the better.

These types of opportunities are always available, and there may be too many for you to engage with. If you do notice an opportunity but recognise that you are not the best person to engage with it, then it is collegial to inform one of your colleagues who may be interested in that type of engagement. After all, you would want them to inform you of an opportunity if they noticed one that could be beneficial to you, right?

These types of engagements can take a lot of time and may not have much direction initially. Action research requires you to embed yourself in a situation, to understand the issue from within and to move towards transformative change. This can be really challenging, and potentially also frustrating, but it can also be rewarding, stimulate a seismic jump forward in your understanding of an important issue and enable you to come up with a new theoretical or empirical contribution to the literature. Engaging with non-academics and policymakers can single you out for a type of learning that many of your colleagues will be avoiding or not prioritising because they do not understand the potential benefits of doing so or are not prepared to take themselves out of their comfort zones to make those non-academic engagements.

Some traditional research leaders do not appreciate the importance of interacting with non-academics and policymakers, perhaps because it does not conform to the training that many experienced. But in today's academic environment, which prioritises impact and, increasingly, knowledge exchange, it is inevitable that these types of interactions become the norm, and research leaders need to actively encourage academics' interactions with non-academics and policymakers.

98. The relevance and impact of your research will evolve, grow and shrink

The importance of research topics to policymakers seems to evolve with fashion: the relevance of particular streams of research will come and go. Some topics seem to remain in the policy arena for much too long, such as the prioritisation of productivity figures,[1] while other topics seem to be consistently deprioritised, like a focused and purposeful reduction in unemployment.

If your research is on a topic that is commonly published in the core journals, you are fortunate, but if your research is on a topic that our colleagues do not consider to be publishable in the core journals, you will need to make a choice. Either you could wait until colleagues and policymakers are interested in your research topic, or you could flirt with other closely connected topics, or you need to accept that your research topic is exceptionally interesting to you but not necessarily as interesting to others at the moment. Rest assured that your research will be of interest to someone, and that the interest and relevance of your work will evolve over time, often in an unpredictable manner.

 Peer effects strongly influence what we all do, what we think is important at a particular time, what we do within contexts and what we prioritise doing. Although you may communicate the importance of your work to policymakers and stakeholders in an effective way, whether they are able to switch their thinking so that they buy-in to the importance of your work depends not only on the strength of your own argument but also on their functional fixity. Being agile enough to recognise the importance of something new within a newly evolving context does demand an extraordinary level of mental agility, and most people's thinking seems to evolve along a path that is dependent on their previous steps. Switching mental recognition of the importance of issues to a new path is unusual and difficult.

Therefore, the ability to make a positive impact on the world is limited by our peers' ability to be swayed by our argument. It may be no fault of your own that your excellent idea is not adopted by a policymaker or another stakeholder. I have been in meetings with senior policymakers who have fully bought into the strength of my argument and would like to fully integrate my ideas into their policymaking. However, their hands have been tied by their more senior and inaccessible colleague(s) who tend to have a particular way of thinking and acting that has proved successful in previous contexts (i.e. in front of their peers). Luckily, at other times, people want to identify a new and innovative idea in order to solve a problem. They may be looking for new ideas to pull themselves out of a desperately poor situation, or they may simply be interested because they have space in their portfolio to do something that is cutting edge.

The number of opportunities that you have to engage with policymakers and stakeholders will change over time due to the perceived relevance and immediacy of your research, but also due to the space that they have to think about, reflect on and prioritise the important work that you recommend to them. Even when you are able to influence a change for the better, that knowledge exchange process may not have an immediate impact, and the longevity of any impact may be short. Opportunities to lever impact can increase or shrink, often associated with your prior reputation and experience, but also through word-of-mouth recommendations. You may need to evolve your own skills or change the way you engage with the outside world.

The evolution of the importance and strength of any academic advice given to policymakers is something that research leaders will know about very well. They will have experienced this evolution themselves when trying to promote their own ideas for change. They also need to be aware of upturns in fashion and opportunities for particular areas of research, and they should bring these areas to the attention of appropriate colleagues.

Research leaders should prioritise exploration into research funding opportunities that are closely linked with their colleagues' research areas, irrespective of the extent to which they recognise, appreciate and understand those areas. This activity is time-consuming and often not recognised in workload models, but early recognition of possible new externally funded research openings is vital for first-mover advantage and to gain impact.

NOTE

1.   See Webber, D. J. (2020), 'Firm-level productivity in two-dimensions', Working Paper, University of Sheffield.

99. Publicise your findings

If your research reveals something that could be interesting not only to your immediate peers but also to a wide range of other academics and business people, actively consider writing for a newspaper or magazine, such as *The Conversation* or *The Economist* or the national press.

If your media piece is accepted, people across the planet may read it, with readership not confined to your immediate discipline. Effective publicity enables you to reach a wide audience and augments your visibility. Together these amplify the potential influence that you could have on policymakers.

Gaining influence through media publicity creates a knowledge exchange function that puts you on a higher platform so that people notice your work more. Those who like your research and what you stand for will take notice and want to work with you; effective publicity may even entice external funding organisations to contact you to undertake some work for them.

Shout from the rooftops.

Barabas and Jerit (2009) emphasise that media coverage increases policy-specific knowledge above and beyond many other factors.[1] The benefit of media coverage is clear and often positive. So why do few academics engage with the media to increase the visibility of their research?

I think the reasons for a lack of engagement with the media vary from one academic to another. Some colleagues suggest that their research has already moved on and therefore they are prioritising new areas. Some colleagues perceive that their main audience is other academics and that Joe Public wouldn't be interested in their research. Other colleagues suggest that it is the media's responsibility to contact them if they are interested in their research. Still other colleagues do not value the benefits of engaging with the media, and for many this would take them far out of their comfort zone.

Attracting those most interested in your research is half the battle to gaining visibility and impact, and should be prioritised for the good of your research and for the potential benefit for society.

Most universities have connections to the media, either indirectly through an agency or directly through someone (or a team) embedded somewhere within the university. They are very aware of the positive benefits of being in the media and emphasise the importance and relevance of ongoing research. Get to know these media people. Research leaders should open channels of communication between those media advocates and their academic colleagues and encourage them to shout about their own research. An excellent first step is to undertake media training in order to become more comfortable talking directly with different types of media.

NOTE

1.   Barabas, J. and Jerit, J. (2009), 'Estimating the causal effects of media coverage on policy-specific knowledge', *American Journal of Policy Science*, 53(1), pp. 73–89.

100. Engage with the media

There are many media outlets open to academics (such as newspapers, radio, television, magazines), but few academics engage with them frequently enough. One reason could be that academics are concerned that their ideas will be misunderstood or twisted to mean something different. Another concern could be that academics recognise that they only have a soundbite to get the complexity of their ideas across in a clear and accurate manner, and that this space is not sufficient. Yet another concern is that the academic will be asked a question that is unrelated to their own research interests or they are put on the spot about something that they do not know about and will therefore appear stupid.

Although these concerns are real, it is also the case that engaging with the media in the right way can have enormous benefits for our research, because it can multiply the size of your audience. There are media training events that you can engage with in order to increase your confidence in media conversations.

I have engaged with several media training events and have learnt something different in every session. Part of this could be because the backgrounds of the media trainers were slightly different, with some trained in radio, some trained in recorded television and others expert in live television. This is one of those areas where you can never have enough training; each one provides guidance and training that can boost your confidence at the microphone. Undertake some media training. It is not only fun, it also puts your mind at rest that you will be okay at it and that it is not something to be afraid of.

Be bold and seize the moment.

 Ensuring that your work is understood by society can empower people and broaden attitudes on particular topics. When engaging with the media, you could interpret the experience as if you are in a different educational situation. For instance, you could see it as an online lecture that enables mass communication with the public.

Engagement with the media enhances the influence that you have on society and boosts the number of people aware of your university department and of the highly relevant research that is undertaken by you and your immediate colleagues. Moreover, it can reduce the impact of, or question, competing views that you think are either misleading or wrong.

You may impress not only prospective students and therefore potentially boost student numbers; you could also entice people to contact you to do some work for them. More opportunities may come your way when other media recognise that you engage with the media process, and especially if they think that you have something interesting to say.

Whenever you have something new to say, perhaps because it has been recently accepted by a peer-reviewed journal, then consider approaching newspapers and magazines that have an interest in your area of research. Engage in radio programmes once you have the confidence and have trained your enthusiasm so that you come across as an inspiring researcher to the listeners. Perhaps even engage in TV shows once you have enough experience. When I undertook one of my first media training sessions back in 2013, the organisation provided me with a book and there was something on page 12 that has stuck in my mind ever since:

> A journalist is not interested in you or your message. The only thing they are interested in is a good story. So make sure you give them something that's interesting that they can use.[1]

Make sure that you know the story that you wish to promote. Know the message that you wish to put across. Provide the soundbite that you wish to give, and practice steering clear of everything else.

Research leaders should encourage all their colleagues, experienced and inexperienced, to participate in media training and engagement. The earlier in their career that they receive this training, the sooner they will feel comfortable at the media microphone. This does not mean that the research leader needs to be in the media very frequently; instead, it means that a research leader should be mindful of the potential benefits that their colleagues could receive should they decide to engage with the media. There is no need for a research leader to insist on such media engagement, but opening doors for their colleagues where relevant and beneficial is what makes a credible and useful research leader.

NOTE

1.   Carter, M. (2012), *Handling the Media*, Mentor Press.

Conclusions

Frequent conversations at conferences and with numerous other colleagues led me to recognise that some academics experience issues at work that demoralise and frustrate them and, they perceive, reduce their ability to achieve their potential. Other colleagues cannot praise their workplaces highly enough for the support they receive and the facilities they have access to, and their personal motivations and achievements are often clear for all to see. These conversations and seemingly correlated disparities in attainments stimulated me to reflect on what could be done in academia to support and enable all academics to achieve their potential. I began to wonder which successful initiatives those colleagues wanted to keep and which initiatives they wanted to implement and adopt to improve some departments' academic cultures, and thereby enable more academics to achieve their research potential. I started making notes of these conversations to enable me to reflect more on their content at a later date but found myself collating so many that I became aware that these issues are far from uncommon; in fact, I realised that there were sufficient issues and corresponding initiatives to write this book.

This book is a collation of those comments, discussions and reflections; some of the ideas and initiatives are individual and personal, while others are department-wide or even institutional. I hope that this discussion of perceptions, reflections and initiatives starts a wider conversation about how we can more actively support researchers across the social sciences to achieve their potential and produce greater amounts of higher-quality research output. This is a collection of ideas that are worth considering for adoption to lead to beneficial change both at a personal level and at a departmental/faculty/institutional level. This book does not present the results of an in-depth research project designed to identify the dynamic implications of particular policies to enhance research, and all points remain up for discussion; but it does present a broad set of initiatives that are considered to work by those who have either employed them or wanted them.

After some essential contextualisation in the Introduction which sets out the need to be civil and supportive at the same time as being constructively critical, the book presents ten sets of ten tips that could lead to academics thriving in their research activities. The main purpose of this text is to encourage us to reflect on how we can collectively and individually make better progress in our research activities. It emphasises that we can achieve more if we work together for mutual gain, and that providing colleagues with support and critical feedback in a reciprocating manner enables us to achieve more and at a faster pace. The development of a collaborative atmosphere encourages colleagues to support (rather than compete with) each other for the good of the department, which stimulates (rather than stifles) greater individual and collective lateral thinking, and may lead to greater amounts of innovation across the economy.

The book has provided a narrative foundation that our research quality will improve when we have the support of our colleagues and when we:

(i)   Are responsible for our own research.
(ii)   Care for and support our colleagues by being fair, conciliatory and empathetic.
(iii)   Contribute proactively to the life of our departments and strive to make them an enjoyable and non-confrontational workplace for all involved.
(iv)   Provide constructively critical feedback to colleagues on their research in attempts to help push their research forward.
(v)   Be helpful and generous to colleagues across our departments by being good citizens.

Providing support is not simply about reminding people that they are doing good research. Support in this context is an enabling characteristic that constructively criticises each other's work in a way that energises and invigorates us to conduct more and better-quality research. Constructive criticism provides specific inspiring and encouraging feedback that is designed to enhance the quality of another person's work, and this type of feedback positively encourages further investigation and reflection. Constructive feedback within a supportive culture does not mislead, degenerate or stunt another person's work in a way that demoralises, belittles or discourages them.

I have argued in this book that working in a culture that feels safe and secure, with mutual respect and support, where we feel able to push our boundaries and make mistakes, and where we are not ridiculed for making an error, but instead are congratulated on having the drive to explore a particular untrodden path with vigour and integrity, will create more innovative research and more successful researchers who themselves have higher levels of job satisfaction. Removing the chains of fear and being assured of support for doing the right thing energises us to conduct detailed and reflective research and will enable us to make more substantive research achievements. Such a culture is set by the research leaders and senior staff, and it is reinforced by colleagues who buy-in to this way of working. There is no undermining, no gaslighting and no fear of retribution in civilised, high-performing academic departments.

I have collated tips, ideas and lessons in this book in the hope of raising awareness that we can purposefully and collectively increase the quality and quantity of our community's research outputs if only we follow a number of community rules that are underpinned by civil interaction and mutual respect. Group-serving behaviour involves sacrifice, and a research leader needs to be efficient enough to make time and space to support their colleagues in an altruistic manner. This is not a win–lose scenario (where the group wins, and the research leader loses); it is a win–win situation: if the profile of the department improves, the profile of the research leader improves. If a research leader is only self-interested, they will lose their colleagues' support and the best colleagues will leave the department.

All universities should possess an environment that generates, sustains and encourages innovation and creativity. My hope is that this text encourages some positive changes in some departments to enable them to develop or deepen such a positive and enabling research culture.

Good luck !!